THE CAVALIER POETS

THE CAVALIER POETS

Their Lives, Their Day, and Their Poetry

BY
CARL HOLLIDAY

Essay Index Reprint Series

BOOKS FOR LIBRARIES PRESS
PLAINVIEW, NEW YORK

First Published 1911

Reprinted 1974

Library of Congress Cataloging in Publication Data

Holliday, Carl, 1879-1936.
   The Cavalier Poets.

   (Essay index reprint series)
   Reprint of the 1911 ed. published by Neale Pub. Co.,
New York.
   Bibliography: p.
   1. English poetry--Early modern (to 1700)--History
and criticism. I. Title.
PR541.H6 1974   821'.008   74-1168
ISBN 0-518-10147-9

To
THAT MODERN CAVALIER POET,
WHO HAS ALL THE MERITS, WITHOUT THE FAULTS,
OF
THE DAINTY METAPHYSICAL SINGERS,
AUSTIN DOBSON

CONTENTS

CONTENTS

PREFACE

Much has been said and written about that dainty, even if artificial, group of seventeenth-century singers known under the various titles of Metaphysical, Cavalier, Rhetorical, Fantastic, and Caroline Poets. Practically every course of study in English literature devotes some space to their happily phrased songs, and innumerable magazine sketches and essays have from time to time reminded us of the bravery and chivalry of these belaced but stout-hearted courtiers. And yet, so far as I am aware, no adequate treatment of this quaint " metaphysical " movement has been attempted in any one book, and, though many of the charming lyrics are popularly known, ideas concerning their origin and their makers are, as a rule, extremely hazy.

This study of the subject is intended for both general readers and students of literature. The lives and works of the most important poets in the group have been discussed, and those selections which seem most characteristic of them and of their day have been presented. And these selections, it is believed, will come to many readers not as strangers, but rather as old friends, doubly welcome now because more intimately understood.

The notes, which need not be numerous, are appreciative rather than technical, and are intended

11

not so much for the student, who usually prefers to
make his own researches, as for the general reader,
who prefers in his poetical readings words for the
heart along with words for the intellect.   In short,
I have endeavored to make this, not an exercise in
philology, but a pleasing and sympathetic *literary*
work. For the "intensive" student, however, I
have added a list of works (with dates) by metaphysical poets, a rather full bibliography, and ref-
erences to the sources of all critical quotations.

I have had some difficulty in settling upon a name
for this quaint choir of singers. As indicated
above, critics have offered at least five titles, and
yet none accurately describes the intangible but distinct personality belonging to the group. Perhaps,
after all, "Cavalier" will serve as well as any; for
though all were not Cavalier in *politics*, all were at
some time in their lives Cavalier in *spirit*. It is my
hope that the sweetness, the daintiness, the chivalry,
the artistic temperament of this spirit may be transmitted in some degree to the readers of this volume,
and that, as they read, they may come to realize
that, after all, life is measured

"In feelings, not in figures on a dial.
We should count time by heart-throbs."

Vanderbilt University,
Nashville, Tennessee.

INTRODUCTION

WHO WERE THE CAVALIER POETS?

There is so much that an introduction, however detailed, cannot make clear — so much of the inner spirit which only the actual writings and lives of the writers can breathe forth. I can but state some reasonably certain facts about the movement with which this study deals; if you would understand what motives moved the group of songsters known as the Cavalier Poets, what and whom they wrote for, why they chose to write in certain characteristic ways, what pleasant bits of daintiness they wrought, you must read the quaint songs themselves, and with them the no less lovable and often heroic lives of those who thus sang so oddly and so melodiously.

Samuel Johnson, with characteristic near-sightedness and bull-headedness, has said of them:

"The metaphysical poets were men of learning, and to show their learning was their whole endeavor: but, unluckily resolving to show it in rhyme, instead of writing poetry they only wrote verse, and very often such verses as stood the trial of the finger better than of the ear; for the modulation was so imperfect that they were only found to be verses by counting the syllables.

13

"If the father of criticism has rightly denominated poetry τέχνη μιμητική, an imitative art, these writers will, without great wrong, lose their right to the name of poets; for they cannot be said to have imitated anything: they neither copied nature nor life; neither painted the forms of matter nor represented the operations of the intellect."[1]

Seldom has criticism been more false. Here the gruff old Doctor seized upon an idea found in Dryden's *Discussion Concerning the Origin and Progress of Satire,* where the "father of English criticism" declares that Dr. Donne, who in part founded this school of singers, "affects the *metaphysics,* . . . and perplexes the minds of the fair sex with nice speculations of philosophy when he should engage their hearts and entertain them with the softness of love." Thereupon the cock-sure Samuel exploited this undoubted defect of Donne and his followers as a salient characteristic, and stretched the name "metaphysical" until it covered nearly all the poets of the earlier seventeenth century who failed to lean toward the Dryden style of poetry.

Various other names have been given these ingenious singers. "Fantastic" is the adjective sometimes applied, and this is not unfair; for surely much that they wrote is pleasingly curious and surprisingly far-stretched. De Quincey has called them the "rhetorical" poets, because of their inventive originality, not in thoughts, but in the manner of joining thoughts; but such a name is hardly comprehen-

[1] *Lives of English Poets:—Cowley.*

sive enough. Still another title given is " Cavalier "; but not all of these men were Royalists. After all, however, " Cavalier " is doubtless the best name; for certainly these songs show the gallantry, the frivolity, the daintiness, the artistic temperament, the light-heartedness, the sentiment and sentimentality, and at times the loyalty and the dashing bravery, of those high-spirited nobles who fought for their king.

But what's in a name? The important questions are: Who were they? Why did they come into existence? What were their poetic ideals? How did they affect English poetry? In order to gain satisfactory answers, let us consider briefly the era and its characteristics.

At the beginning of the seventeenth century the Renaissance in England had largely spent its vigor; the thrilling enthusiasm of the Elizabethan times had passed. Then came the studied morality of James, and a little later the studied immorality of Charles. The English mind seems to have assumed that decorum, restraint, and demand for stately formalities which often characterize a hypocritical sinner, and there now arose quibbles over artistic trifles which the Elizabethan genius magnanimously ignored. Yet, I would not leave the impression that the island had become a hotbed of secret immorality and outward punctiliousness. In spite of the fact that song was frequently indecent and the stage worse, there was being written much that is looked upon to-day as deeply, sincerely devotional.

But such literature, praiseworthy in its heartfulness, is not eminently true to its day.

Now, in the opening years of the seventeenth century the younger verse-writers came under the influence of two poets of undeniable talents — Ben Jonson and Dr. John Donne. And back of both was another influence, remote but very real — that of Spenser. But Spenser lacked self-restraint; so long as the song was lovely he was entirely willing to let it wander on forever. Some one was needed to teach limitation, conciseness, intense condensation, and that one came in the person of rare Ben Jonson. Precision of diction, daintiness, freedom from rambling, dislike for scattered thoughts and hazy figures of speech — these were the prime characteristics of the huge play-writer, the very traits that have gained him lasting praise. Thus to the Spenserian beauty was added artistic economy. And then came Donne, a delver in the realm of the abstract, a poet who loved to choose his rhetorical figures from mystical philosophy, from mediæval lore, from remote sciences, from forgotten theologies — in short, from the realm of the metaphysical.

The time was now ripe, and the new school appeared. Its singers adored beauty; they were brief; they sought afar for their " conceits." The result was a poetry with more fancy than imagination, more art than emotion, more cleverness than inspiration. The stretched figure known as the " conceit," which Johnson seized upon as a criterion of the metaphysical, was, indeed, used to a ruinous ex-

tent; and yet it was but one trait, and not always
the most noticeable one at that. Be it remembered,
too, that when it was used it was by no means always
a detriment. At times, indeed, it rose by its originality, daring, and lofty conception into the very
kingdom of noble literature itself. Is there not
something startling in the famous conceit of
Vaughn's *World?*

  " I saw Eternity the other night
    Like a ring of pure and endless light
      All calm as it was bright;
    And round beneath it, Time, in hours, days, years,
      Driven by the spheres,
    Like a vast shadow moved, in which the world
      And all her train were hurled."

Donne has been mentioned as fostering this far-
fetched comparison, the conceit; in fact, he has been
accused of giving it such popularity as to entitle
him to the name of "father of the metaphysical
school." Perhaps it would be well, therefore, to
pause at this point, and consider who this once admired poet was.

Thomas Campbell has declared that the life of
John Donne is more interesting than his poetry,[2]
and Campbell is right; for in this man's little span
of years we find condensed the tragedy of human
existence — the frivolities, the sins, the repentance,
the earnest striving for a Godlike righteousness. A
ghastly white marble image of him stands in a dark

[2] *Specimens of the British Poets.*

niche of St. Paul's, and in that chiseled stone we
read the story of a soul worn by struggles with its
own passions. In his earlier days he was " a great
visitor of ladies, a great frequenter of plays, a
great writer of conceited verses"; but as the years
passed he " became so rare a preacher that he was
not only commended, but even admired by all who
heard him." [3] To us of to-day it seems strange
that the greatest wit of a licentious court should
have become one of the most brilliant, zealous, and
godly divines of the English Church.

He was born in London, in 1573, of Catholic
parents, and was a direct descendant of the famous
Sir Thomas More. At about the age of ten he entered Hart Hall, Oxford University, passed in 1587
to Trinity College, Cambridge, and showed scholarly
ability in both institutions, but received no degree.
He was a wanderer on the Continent from 1588 to
1590, and a little later became a student of law at
Lincoln's Inn, London. For some reason, however,
he did not succeed at anything, and therefore it was
perhaps very fortunate that his father's death at
this time made him the possessor of three thousand
pounds. Now, for a space, his career is a little
hazy, and perhaps it is well. We know that in 1592
or 1593 he became a Protestant; we know that he
was rapidly squandering the small fortune be-
queathed him; we have evidences that he was gaining
some reputation as a poet; and we know that in 1594
he took once more to his continental wanderings.

[3] Sir Richard Baker, *Chronicle of the Kings of England.*

From this time forth the story grows more definite. He was in the service of the Earl of Essex at Cadiz in January, 1596, and from August of that year he was secretary to Sir Thomas More.

Now came a crisis in his life. He fell madly in love with Anna More, daughter of the lord-lieutenant of the Tower and niece of Sir Thomas More, and secretly married her. For this he was dismissed from the service of Sir Thomas, and was thrown into the Tower. Liberty soon came, however, and for a time he lived with relatives at various country-places, spending his enforced leisure in wide study and writing. And results began to be evident. He completed his *Satires* and *The Progress of the Soul;* in 1602 ten sonnets, addressed to Philomel, appeared in Davison's *Poetical Rhapsody;* other verses soon followed. Steadily, too, he was gaining favor at Court. In 1610 Oxford conferred the M. A. upon him; in 1611 he was requested to accompany Sir Robert Drury to Paris on government business; in that same year the appearance of his *Anatomy of the World* brought him wide notice. Now came the royal pressure upon him to enter the Church. James would listen to no excuses; all offices outside the priesthood were refused the poet. Lover of the world though he was, Donne buckled down to his theology, was ordained in January, 1615, was offered fourteen good livings, became chaplain to the king, in 1615 received the D. D. from Cambridge at His Majesty's request, was made rector of Keystone in January, 1616, and of Sevenoaks in July,

1616, and became Divinity Reader to Lincoln's Inn before the close of the year. Surely, success was his.

The wife for whom he had formerly suffered so much died in 1617, and for a time the good doctor was inconsolable. For a year or more he lived a rather secluded life in Germany; but England was in need of earnest men, and in 1620 we find him Dean of St. Paul's. Honors now came thick and fast. In 1622 he was made rector of Blunham, in 1623 vicar of St. Dunstan-in-the-West, and the same year prolocutor to convocation. This rapid rise of the versatile churchman is not to be wondered at; for he was loved by multitudes. Says Izaak Walton: " The melancholy and pleasant humor were in him so contempered that each gave advantage to the other and made his company one of the delights of mankind. . . . His aspect was cheerful and such as gave a silent testimony of a clear knowing soul and of a conscience at peace with itself. His melting eye showed that he had a soft heart, full of noble compassion; of too brave a soul to offer injuries, and too much a Christian not to pardon them in others . . . and of so merciful a spirit that he never beheld the miseries of mankind without pity and relief." [4]

Surely old Walton was right in his belief in the poet-priest's moral beauty; for when Donne's last hours drew near he showed his disdain for death by wrapping himself in his winding-sheet and having

[4] *Life of Dr. John Donne.*

his portrait painted thus. The soul went its way on the last day of March, 1631, and the dust was entombed in St. Paul's, where the white image stands to-day. And the king, ever his friend, wrote a poem *To the Memory of My Ever Desired Friend, Doctor Donne*:

> " At common graves we have poetic eyes
> Can melt themselves in easy elegies . . . .
> But at thine, poem or inscription
> (Rich soul of wit and language) we have none.
> Indeed, a silence does that tomb befit,
> When is no Herald left to blazon it."

Some of these men of the seventeenth century lived the strenuous life as heartily as we of to-day live it. Donne is an excellent instance. The list of his printed works is astonishing in its length. Only a few need be mentioned: The *Satires*, the *Progress of the Soul*, and the sonnets already spoken of, *Pseudo-Martyr* (1610); *Anatomy of the World* (1611); a great number of sermons, *Death's Duel* (1630); and after death, *Poems by John Donne* (1633); *Juvenilia* (1633); *Essays in Divinity* (1651); *Paradoxes, Problems, Essays* (1652); *Donne's Satyr* (1662); and at length the practically complete *Poetical Works*, edited by Izaak Walton, in 1679.

This, then, was the so-called father of the metaphysical school. His life is characteristic of the lives of the various singers in that school. All were men of culture; all led lives of intense activity; nearly all made great sacrifices for their ruler; all snatched moments from the very teeth of Time to sing in brief but melodious strains. Dr. Donne's songs received in the old days excessive praise; Dryden lauded them, and everybody knew of them. And yet they seem oftentimes to be but harsh and crabbed verses. Earnestness of thought we do not deny him, but the form of the thought is so odd, so fantastic. We can see the poet's insight into the spiritual life; but we can see no less clearly the far-fetched imagery, the long search for odd comparisons, the dusty relics of forgotten learning — in other words, the *metaphysics*.

Now, as to that other singer who apparently affected the metaphysical school. When Ben Jonson died in 1637 all England mourned the loss. The first poet to be recognized as Poet-Laureate, a literary dictator during the last decade of his life, a skilful manipulator of harmonious phrases, withal, a man of rough but sincere nature, he wielded over his century an influence never granted an English writer of previous days. A few months after his death there appeared a volume of poetical praise of him, entitled *Jonsonus Virbius*, and many a famous man of the times prided himself that he had placed a stanza or two within the book. Authors now delighted in calling themselves " sons of Ben," and in their admiration imitated not a few of his virtues. Poets grew more careful of the form and the length of their songs; they displayed their learning well; they introduced frequent philosophical and satirical touches. Their counter-admiration for Dr. Donne, however, caused them to lack rare Ben's reserve in the use of unusual figures of speech, and the result was that, imitating Donne's often successful efforts in conceit-raking, they frequently fell far short of good taste and made themselves ridiculous. Indeed, these conceits sometimes arouse disgust in their most sympathetic modern readers. Thus, at length, this constant search for new comparisons made some of these poets heedless of the very trait which at first they had so greatly admired in Jonson — perfect symmetry — and their songs degenerated at times into downright slovenliness. But, in general, it may be said that their work represents a reaction from the rhetorical and verse freedom of the Elizabethans.

Undoubtedly these poets were intellectually of a superior class. Intellectuality, in fact, often took the place of real emotion — a characteristic traceable in part to Donne — and cleverness, it seems, was more to be desired than depth of truth. These men did not take poetry seriously enough. Jonson made a life-work of it; but the Cavalier singers were courtiers, soldiers, or clergymen first, and poets whenever they had a spare moment. Too often their works but press home the fact that they desired only to display their skill in dainty jugglery. Yet what pleasant jugglery it is! Doubt their motives and their sincerity as we may, we must admit their surprisingly true lyrical quality. A veritable nest of song-birds they were; the question, however, is whether you prefer the tamed canary-bird or the wild mocking-bird. We must not think that in their word-juggling they continually used a distorted style. See how the words of sweet-voiced Herrick's *To Daffodils* flow — so naturally, with so little inversion, with that child-like simplicity which only real artistic genius can assume:

> " We have short time to stay as you,
>   We have as short a spring;
> As quick a growth to meet decay
>   As you or anything.
>   We die
> As your hours do, and dry
>   Away,
> Like to the summer's rain;
> Or as the pearls of morning's dew,
>   Ne'er to be found again."

There is frequently a flippant worldliness of tone in these Cavalier lyrics; but not always. *Vers de Societe* flourished, of course, for it is an outgrowth of a highly artificial social life, and the days of James and Charles were anything but natural. And there is a certain pleasure in such verse, even if my lady-love is not expected to trust implicitly in its declarations:

> " Bid me despair, and I'll despair,
>   Under that cypress tree;
> Or bid me die, and I will dare
>   E'en death, to die for thee."

But it must ever be remembered that there were hundreds of these belaced Cavaliers as deeply re-

ligious as any Roundhead that ever twanged a psalm.
Professor Felix Schelling expresses it well when he
says: " A superficial consideration of this century is
apt to divide all England into the hostile camps of
Roundhead and Cavalier; to consider all the former
hypocrites and all the latter as good loyal men; or
. . . to believe all supporters of the king utterly
misguided and to assume that all the virtuous flourished in the Puritan party alone." [5] These metaphysical poets did not always choose the frivolous
as a theme; at times their subjects touch the noblest
emotions of mankind. Herrick, earth-lover as he
was, tuned some heartfelt songs of thanksgiving;
Cowley was grandly moral; Herbert was absolutely
puritanical in his self-questioning; Crashaw scaled
heaven with ecstatic rhapsodies. But as a *general*
criticism it may be stated that the metaphysical
group made a rather sharp distinction between
earthly beauty and heavenly beauty, and that they
had a very human preference for the former.

Who, then, were the Metaphysical Poets? What
definition may be given of them? They were a group
of lyrical poets of the earlier seventeenth century
who, with considerable attention to form, sang generally, but not always, of the lighter phases of
earthly love, and who in their singing made such use
of hyperbole, strained metaphors, and the other far-
fetched figures known as " conceits," as to suggest
a state of mind which may with some fairness be
called " metaphysical."

[5] *Seventeenth Century Lyrics*, p. 58.

Why did they pass away? Well, it is hard to give precise reasons for any literary change, but certain modifying influences may generally be discerned. As the years of the second half of the seventeenth century passed, true lyrics became more and more scarce. The range of poetic subjects and of poetic vision grew more restricted. Enthusiasm became akin to crime. The healthful restrictions that Jonson had instituted had now become unhealthful in their narrowness. Occasional subjects largely took the place of general, world-wide, universal themes. The day of Pope's reserved, glittering style was approaching. Many of the Cavalier singers had now gone to the grave, and of the others, those who had not thrown themselves into the struggles of the Commonwealth were content to retire to the privacy of the study or to the seclusion of the Church.

Various other reasons for the decline of the movement have been given. Gosse holds that one of the songsters, who was metaphysical in his early work — Edmund Waller — evolved the new style of poetry, known as the classical, out of his clever inner consciousness;[6] others believe that George Sandys, a brilliant courtier of the hour, founded the new movement; while others declare that the idea had crept in from France and was breathed in with the English air. The last theory is, very likely, near the truth; for the return of Charles II, while it brought a deal of vile wickedness, infused a certain stiffness, for-

[6] *Eighteenth Century Literature*, p. 2.

mality, and cold brilliance into the social life of the day, and, naturally, poetry voiced the tone of the life about it.

Be all this as it may, the fact remains that the metaphysical poets passed almost as quickly and as silently as they had come, and for a time it seemed that their influence had completely perished with them. But there was too much sweetness, beauty, worth in that group to merit such a fate. Here and there during the classical period a timid, slender-voiced lyrist kept alive the spirit of real song, nourished and transmitted it, until at last it burst forth into the full-voiced chorus of the Romantic Movement, the passionate music of Burns, Byron, and Shelley. The influence of that passing choir of seventeenth-century singers is still evident. Among the younger writers of England there seems to be some revival of the spirit that moved Herrick and Suckling and Lovelace, and to-day Austin Dobson stands for all that was best in the Cavalier poets, with all their daintiness and genius for form, without their excessive love for remote resemblances. In America a multitude of minor poets bear testimony to the perseverance of the best principles of Cavalier song. Especially has this been true of the verse-writers of the Southern States, where John Shaw, William Maxwell, Richard Henry Wilde, Philip Pendleton Cooke, James Legare, Samuel Minturn Peck, and many others have composed melodious trifles to innumerable lovely maidens. The verse found in the magazines of America to-day shows that the numerous amateurs in song find something decidedly attractive in the concise, dainty, and ever lovable lyrics of the old days of rouge and lace. It is a tendency to be encouraged; for lyrical gems are a solace to the heart and a grateful gift to posterity. That they are not mighty-lined epics is no cause for sneers; the violet is as perfect a plant as the palm-tree.

> " It is not growing like a tree
>   In bulk, doth make men better be;
> Or standing long an oak, three hundred year,
> To fall a log at last, dry, bald, and sear:
>   A lily of a day
>   Is fairer far, in May,
>   Although it fall and die that night;
>   It was the plant and flower of light.
> In small proportions we just beauties see;
> And in short measures life may perfect be."

THE LEADERS

WHAT MANNER OF MEN THEY WERE

ROBERT HERRICK

(1591 — 1674)

" Gather ye rosebuds while ye may,
   Old time is still a-flying;
And this same flower that smiles to-day
   To-morrow will be dying."

We all have heard it before — the famous old
song; but how many of us have reached back through
the centuries, grasped the singer's hand, and learned
to know him as a friend? Twelve hundred such
songs he wrote, many of them just as beautiful,
none of them without charm. And yet this man Herrick was but a country clergyman, almost neglected
by the great and witty, and bitterly complaining at
times of his exile from the dear, laughter-ringing
inns of noisy London. Life flowed smoothly with
Robert Herrick, smoothly as the meadow brooks in
his ancient Devonshire parish, and that was the reason of his discontent. He admitted that he wrote
more and better poetry than he would have written
had he been amidst the beloved roar of the metropolis; but, then,— well, who can deny the fascination,
the thrill, of a throbbing city? Well for him, however, that Fortune was temporarily unkind to him;
for Time has crowned him the most versatile singer
of them all. What freshness is here, what ingenious

31

turns of thought, what a multitude of subjects!
It was no idle boast of his to say:

"I sing of brooks, of blossoms, birds, and bowers,
Of April, May, of June, and July-flowers;
I sing of May-poles, hock-carts, wassails, wakes,
Of bridegrooms, brides, and of their bridal-cakes.
I write of Youth, of Love;—and have access
By these, to sing of cleanly wantonness;
I sing of dews, of rains, and, piece by piece,
Of balm, of oil, of spice, and ambergris.
I sing of time's trans-shifting; and I write
How roses first came red, and lilies white.
I write of groves, of twilights, and I sing
The court of Mab, and of the Fairy King.
I write of Hell; I sing and ever shall
Of Heaven—and hope to have it after all."[1]

Is there not a cheeriness about all this? It is
characteristic of our hearty country parson; for he
drank the wine of life deeply and gladly. He was a
rough-looking fellow—he had the aspect of one
meditating assault and battery, Thomas Bailey Aldrich declares; but to offset the picture there is much
indirect testimony to the amiability of the man,
aside from the evidence furnished by his own writings.[2] "This Robert Herrick was a ponderous,
earthy-looking man with huge double chin, drooping
cheeks, a great Roman nose, prominent glassy eyes,
that showed around them the red lines begotten of
strong potions of Canary, and the whole set upon a
massive neck which might have been that of Helioga-

[1] *Argument of the Hesperides.*
[2] Introduction to Herrick's *Poems,* p. 28.

balus. It was such a figure as the artist would make — typical of a man who loves the grossest pleasures." [3]

He was the son of a Cheapside goldsmith, who fell (purposely, his pastor claimed) from an upper window of his dwelling, and died from the effects of his injuries, leaving his widow and children a small fortune. Robert Herrick thus had the opportunity of securing a good education, but little more. We know that he attended Westminster School, was bound an apprentice to his uncle in 1607, and in 1613 was a student in St. John's College, Cambridge. We know, too, that like all college boys he was constantly complaining of lack of funds, and that he even wrote his uncle that he was hampered in his pursuit of knowledge by want of money to pay teachers and to buy books. In 1616 he removed to Trinity Hall, in order that expenses might be lower and that he might have opportunities in the study of law, and there he obtained his B. A., in 1617, and undertook in a desultory way some of the requirements of the Master's degree.

And now we come to some ten or twelve years the record of which is rather hazy; and perhaps it is best, for in those wild days of Ben Jonson men lived furiously. O rare Ben Jonson! How strangely the big-hearted fellow influenced the dreamers of his day! Herrick met him — at the first performance of the *Alchemist*, in 1610, it is said — and was ever

[3] Mitchell's *English Lands, Letters, and Kings, Elizabeth to Anne*, p. 124.

afterwards an admiring, grateful "son of Ben."
The joyous view of life taken by Jonson, the fays
and elves of his dainty masques, the simple beauty
of his lyrics, above all, the sympathetic, brimming
soul of the burly dramatist — all these appealed to
Herrick's genial nature, and his heart never forgot.
Years later the memory of these riotous days brought
the flush to his cheek.   He cries:

> "Ah, Ben!
> Say how or when
> Shall we, thy guests,
> Meet at those lyric feasts."

Thus Herrick passed the years, at times in peaceful Cambridge, at times in gay London, until in October, 1629, he went to Dean Prior in Devonshire
to show the rustics the way to heaven.   How much
more aptly he might have shown them the way to
the noisiest ale-house in London!   But, after all, it
is surprising — and gratifying — to see how quickly
these seventeenth-century rakes reformed and became
not only serious men but sincerely devout Christians.
Robert Herrick, the happy-go-lucky friend of happy
Ben and many another London wit, grew to be at
least one of the most sympathetic clergymen in all
England.   True it is, however, that he was

> "Of wicked wit by no means chary —
> Of ruddy lips not at all afraid;
> If you gave him milk in a Devonshire dairy,
> He'd probably kiss the dairy maid." [4]

[4] Mortimer Collins' *Herrick*.

In the main, his parishioners were a rough crowd, "rude almost as rudest savages," he himself declared, and doubtless his soul was often vexed. In fact, tradition says that one Sunday morning, finding them inattentive, he threw his sermon at them, and drove them with curses from the church. Perhaps he had been thinking at breakfast that morning of the dear, savory inns of old London! A man like Herrick, however, could but take a healthy view of any kind of existence, and we find him discovering pleasure in many a little thing. Weeks, yes, months he spent teaching a pet pig to drink from a tankard, and then invited his rustic neighbors in to see the exhibition. He found Devonshire old-fashioned enough to have May-poles and other ancient sports, and in the encouragement of these and in the idealizing of them he found a quiet sort of joy. His faithful housemaid, "Prewdence Baldwin," whose name he has given some fame in his verses, kept his little home in order, and life for him contained much peace. Removed from occasions of mental dissipation, with little to disturb his long days, with abounding health, and with picturesque scenery on every side, he wrote with an ease, a freshness, and a frequency that, as he admitted, far surpassed what he would have done at "the Sun, the Dog, and the Triple Tun." Every poet needs a dreamland, and this was his. "Herrick alone, with imperturbable serenity, continued to pipe out his pastoral ditties and crown his head with daffodils when England was torn to pieces with the most momentous struggle for

liberty in her annals . . . . People were invited
to listen to little madrigals upon Julia's stomacher
at the singularly inopportune moment when the eyes
of the whole nation were bent on the unprecedented
phenomenon of the proclamation of an English re-
public." [5]

But in 1647 there came a rude shock. The
Roundheads were in power, and the genial Herrick
was ejected as a Royalist. Back to London he went
— gladly went back, wrote an enthusiastic poem entitled *His Return to London*, and in his *Farewell to
Dean Bourn* declared that he would return to the
parish when " rocks turn to rivers, rivers turn to
men." He settled in Westminster, and, as he had
several wealthy relatives, doubtless did not suffer for
ready money. Again there is a hazy interval. What
is one poor little individual in teeming London — especially if he be only a poet and not a haberdasher?
We know only that in August, 1662, one Robert
Herrick was restored to his parish at Dean Prior;
nor he did he wait, it seems, for rocks to turn to
rivers and rivers to men. Little enough we have of
him from this time on. In the deep-shaded graveyard of Dean Prior there is a stone with the words:
" Robert Herrick, October 15, 1674."

That inconvenient but inevitable affair of death
worried Herrick. He loved life intensely; he found
his dreams so pleasant, he gained such joy from sky
and tree and flower, one cannot censure his reluc-
tance to go. He was " the Ariel of fools, ' sucking

[5] Gosse's *Seventeenth Century Studies*, p. 114.

where the bee sucks,' from the rose-heart of nature,
and reproducing the fragrance idealized." [6]   Years
before his final hour he wrote a little song to death
— a song full of childlike timidity, beginning:

> " Thou bidd'st me come away,
> And I'll no longer stay
> Than for to shed some tears
> For faults of former years."

How often, in the midst of play, that shadow
comes over him! Hedonist that he is, finding a sensuous delight in wine and fruit, flower and tree,
maidenhood and rustic virility, he detests the sad
images that *will* come in spite of all — the images of
the dark pall and the narrow house. " To Herrick,"
says Professor Hale, " the two greatest things of
life were Love and Death — and his mind turned
constantly to the thought of one or the other." [7]
At times he makes a woful attempt to assume a bold
face before the grim messenger, as in *His Winding
Sheet*, where he names the many advantages of
death.   But, somehow, nature will out, and then he
cries:

> " O Time, that cut'st down all,
> And scarce leav'st here
> Memorial
> Of any men that were! "

In every flower, in every dew-drop, aye, and in
every maiden, he saw the temporariness of life. Is

[6] Elizabeth Barrett Browning's *The Book of the Poets.*
[7] Edition of Herrick, p. 36.

it any wonder that such a nature resolved to seize
the pleasure of every fleeting moment? How much
of joy he could discover in the little things of life!
His muse was not above participating in the mixing
of a wedding-cake, the decking of a May-pole, the
preparations for a country dance. Indeed, to this
sophisticated age his use of ordinary things seems
to verge on the ridiculous. He does not hesitate to
write a verse or two about his " teeming hen " which
lays her egg each day, his ewes which bear twins
each year, his goose, which with a jealous ear,

> " Lets loose
> His tongue to tell what danger's near."

In short, he is rather interested in his pig and hen
and goose, and thinks every one else will be; and he
is about right, for all the world loves a lover, even
if he be but a lover of pigs and hens and geese. A
simple, kindly, sin-forgiving man, never a deep
thinker, but a despiser of shams, he rather smiled
upon the meaningless sports of the rustic folk, and
joined heartily in grasping the fragmentary gifts
of close-fisted Time.

Such a man would do all in his power to trans-
form a pleasing sensation into a subtle, delicious
pleasure. Without doubt the rustics about Dean
Prior were rough, clumsy, sensual creatures, huge
eaters, piggish drinkers and prolific breeders; but
lo! Herrick idealized his clodhoppers, as they tum-
bled about the May-pole, and they became Greek
shepherds dancing to Pan's music. He made the

world a dreamland — and what other way is there of being happy? Says Edmund Gosse: "He was an exile from Arcadia all his days, walking through our sober modern life without revolt or passion, but always conscious that he had seen more glorious sights, and walked through a land much more eminent for luxury and beauty." For his was a pagan turn of mind, and he seemed really to long for an age in which he might garland some woodland idol and pour out a cup of wine before it. Preacher though he was, he often in vision saw the little vicarage turn to a columned hall of antique worship, and heard, instead of the crooning song of the housemaid, Prudence, the lofty chant of the Greek choristers singing before some now forgotten god. Yet, as we have seen, he was a good clergyman and wrote orthodox sermons and devout songs to the One God. But how lacking he was in the grave earnestness of Herbert's meditations and the vastness of Milton's conceptions! Lover of the ancient that he was, his fancy took the place of religious fervor, and he sang to God as to Apollo.

Now and then, however, he sounded a true devotional note. His was not a deep, passionate nature, but, given some little event in his own round of life or some picturesque episode from the scriptural record, he could sing with sweetness and with earnestness. Read his *Dirge for Jepthah's Daughter* and hear the Hebrew virgins chant like Greek shepherdesses. Or, better still, sing with him that lowly and human "farmer's hymn" which he called *A Thanks-*

giving to God for His House. Truly, as Saintsbury has said, there is nothing in English verse to equal the *Thanksgiving* as an expression of religious trust.[8]

Kind, quickly forgiving soul, he was too easily satisfied, however, with this earth to rise very far above it. Why strive to sound a mighty anthem to God when he could indite such dainty lyrics to Venus or Julia? He knew so little of the world to come, and this one was so beautiful!

After all, his exile in " loathed Devonshire " gave him his chief charms — his love of abounding life and his ever-quickening love of Nature and her creatures. What open-air freshness and country freedom are here! The " Nature " of which he sang knew nothing of the hotbeds of a London palace; these plants were never potted. Herrick could afford to be unconventional, to roam at leisure through the wide meadows and the wooded uplands, for life about Dean Prior was sane and healthful, even if a little crude. " Thus he was preserved from that public riot and constant disturbance of the commonwealth which did its best to drown the voice of every poet from Carew to Dryden, which drove Crashaw away to madness and death, which made harsh the liquid melodies of Milton, which belied the promise of Davenant and broke the heart of Cowley." [9] It is for this reason that he reflects so little the bitterness and turmoil of his time. While Sir John Suckling casts a cynical leer at the grandees of the court, while Lovelace

---

[8] *History of Elizabethan Literature,* p. 356.
[9] Edmund Gosse, in Ward's *English Poets,* Vol. II, p. 125.

swears eternal love to queenly ladies of rouge and
powder, Herrick is down on his knees in a field of
daffodils, softly whispering to them:

> "Fair daffodils, we weep to see
> You haste away so soon."

He spoke of Nature, not because it was the fad
at court, but because, in his simple-minded way, he
loved her. Carew's flowers may be of the most elegant kind of scented paper, but Herrick's sparkle
with the dew-drops fresh from the garden. Oh, how
the world loves a man of red blood! Laces and scarlet coats may blind for a little time; but, after all,
life — spontaneous, surging life — fascinates mankind. And Herrick saw so much of it about him
in the glowing fields of Devonshire. We know him,
therefore, as a lover of physical beauty — perhaps
dangerously so, as some of his unsavory verses would
indicate; for deep down in his heart he believed that
"few beads are best when once we go a-Maying."
Life was to him at times an intoxication.

When we read the songs of many of Herrick's contemporaries, we are weighed down with heavy odors
— the stuffy plush and velvets, the deep carpets and
tapestry. But here at Dean Prior how full of sunshine! One catches the flavor of ripening fruit
hanging over the sunlit wall, sees the singing har-
vesters raking in the yellow fields, hears the low of
the cattle down by the widening brook. There is a
quiet sort of suppressed passion in it all; no storm,

it is true, but rather the sunny skies of morning and
the ruddy glow of the sunset.

Thus, while others wasted their powers in riotous
revelry, he of necessity glided through his quiet days,
guarding every resource and taking time to convert
every song into a gem. He was not unambitious,
and yet he seemed to write more for himself than for
fame and applause. Even his complimentary verse
to the nobility shows none of that craving for admiration such as one may find so easily in other
lyricists of his age. He published, it seems, but two
collections, the *Hesperides*, of 1648, and the *Noble
Numbers*, dated 1647, and the readers of the day
knew him better perhaps through his contributions
to such hodge-podge collections as " *Wit's Recrea-
tion, Wit's Interpreter, The Academy of Compliments* and *The Mysteries of Love and Eloquence*.
Wonderful books were they — wonderful in their
strange mixtures, wonderful in the amount of cleverness hidden between their lids. That Herrick's was
pretty successfully hidden is evident; for he was almost completely forgotten until that keen-eyed in-
vestigator, Nichols, praised him in the *Gentleman's
Magazine* of 1796. The reason is plain. Genius
though he was, Herrick affected his immediate suc-
cessors far less than did Carew, Suckling, and
Waller; for these men were in the line of movement
toward the cold and brilliant " classic " school,
while Herrick stood aside, tuned his healthy song,
and had to bide his time.

And yet, compare them all, and who sang so ten-

derly, so simply, so naturally, so personally, so originally as Robert Herrick? His was

> " The sparkling rhyme
> That, like a dimple in an old dame's chin,
> Laughs out at Time." [10]

When we read that famous lyric,

> "Gather ye rosebuds while ye may,
> Old time is still a-flying,"

we instantly ask, " Why had not some one else said
that long before? " The lines are so frank, so utterly unforced. So, too, are the verses *To Anthea:*

> " Bid me to live, and I will live
> Thy protestant to be."

Every poem is complete, rounded, so artlessly said,
and yet with what supreme art! The modern Jap-
anese hold the Poe idea — that a poem should be
short, and should express with supreme terseness and
happiness one fleeting sentiment — and our modern
magazines are forcing the verse-writers of the day to
this same conclusion. Long ago Herrick grasped
the idea, and what polished gems resulted!

Space will not allow a discussion of his numerous
poetical virtues: smoothness — hear it in his *Hymn to
Love;* quaintness — see it in the *Prayer to Ben Jon-*

[10] Welch, *In an Ancient Copy of Herrick's Hesperides, Century,* Vol. LVII, p. 477.

son; originality — note it in *To Electra* and *To Dianeme.* Many, many were his metrical experiments, and in all we find a liquid flow of words and a happy recurrence of rhyme; the songs sing themselves. What more may one say? In quantity, spontaneity, verbal music, he shines forth above the other song-writers of his century, while perhaps in all English literature he is excelled in the lyric quality by Burns and Shelley only.

Robert Herrick is a man to love. He takes you into his confidence. A certain personal note gives his verses at times a tinge of pathos — not the wild, heartbroken pathos of Burns, but a subdued, tender regret that life is so short and that we must all go.

He is an egoist; he does not hesitate to mention his own name. "Here, here the tomb of Robin Herrick is," he whispers in *Robin Red-Breast.*

> "Make the way smooth for me,
>   When I, thy Herrick,
>   Honoring thee on my knee
>   Offer my lyric,"

he prays to Ben Jonson. And he complains in *The Loss of His Mistresses:*

> "All are gone,
>   Only Herrick's left alone."

He tells us of Julia and all his other loves, and even though they were but creatures of his dreams, we sorrow with him when they frown and rejoice with

him when they smile. Is that not triumph enough
for a lover and a poet? Surely his songs will live
as long as the world has a sighing lover to read
them — and after that we shall need no poetry.

"Many suns have set and shone,
  Many springs have come and gone,
  Herrick, since thou sang'st of Wake,
  Morris-dance, and Barley-break;
  Many men have ceased from care,
  Many maidens have been fair,
  Since thou sang'st of Julia's eyes,
  Julia's lawns and tiffonies;
  Many things are past — but thou,
  Golden-Mouth, art singing now,
  Singing clearly as of old,
  And thy numbers are of gold." [11]

[11] Austin Dobson, *In a Copy of the Lyrical Poems of Robert Herrick, Scribner*, Vol. I, p. 66.

FRANCIS QUARLES

(1592 — 1644)

" Milton was forced to wait until the world had done admiring Quarles." So says Horace Walpole.[1] Great in Cavalier days was the now forgotten poet's fame. Forgotten? No, not quite. To-day in scattered cotter's homes in rural England Quarles' *Divine Emblems,* with its quaint old cuts by Marshall, is still to be found, and even yet on Sunday afternoon the venerated volume is read by the ancient folk of the household. That gruff Scotchman, James Beattie, writing in 1776, put it too bluntly when he said of Quarles and Blackmore that bad writing could be found anywhere in them; " but as nobody reads their works, nobody is liable to be misled by them." [2] Hear what our own American, Thoreau, wrote to Mrs. Emerson three-quarters of a century later: "I think you would like him," he says. " It is rare to find one who was so much of a poet and so little of an artist. . . . Hopelessly quaint, as if he lived all alone and knew nobody but his wife, who appears to have reverenced him. He never doubts his genius; it is only he and his God in all the world. He uses language sometimes as greatly as Shakespeare; and though there is not

[1] *Letters,* Ed. Cunningham, Vol. III, p. 99.
[2] *Essay on Poetry and Music.*

much straight grain in him, there is plenty of tough, crooked timber."

And so there is; and it would have been splendid timber for a Puritan meeting-house, too. As we read the pious meditations of this "voluminous saint"[3] we, who have read the conventional text-books on history, can but wonder that he is called a Cavalier. How often the thought is impressed upon us by the pedagogues that the Cavalier was a boastful, deep-drinking, loud-swearing, lace-adorned swaggerer; and how erroneous the idea! Many of them were good men — good enough, indeed, to believe that God did not despise a May-pole or a rustic dance. Here, in Francis Quarles, is a gentleman, thoughtful, moral, a steady man of family — he had eighteen children — a lover of things of good report, an earnest believer in his religion, a genuine praise-maker of God. Cromwell could not have been ashamed to put him at the very head of his psalm-singing and God-fearing Ironsides. Let us glance at his unusually calm life of thought and song.

He was born at Romford, Essex, of a family of some importance in the government service. The father died early in life, leaving fifty pounds a year to the boy. After attending a country school, he entered Christ's College, Cambridge — how many a famous man has heard the lectures there! — and received his B. A. in 1608. He decided to be a lawyer, and to this end entered Lincoln's Inn; but that he was more in love with harmony than with discord is

[3] Campbell, *Specimens of the British Poets.*

evidenced by the fact that he sold his law-gowns to
buy a lute-case. One might perpetrate a very
truthful pun by insinuating that it was practically
the only case he ever secured. Already the young
fellow was something of a Puritan in his thoughts
and actions, often declaring that he despised the
glittering court-life of the day; and yet when he was
offered the honor of cup-bearer to the Princess
Elizabeth on her marriage to the Elector-Pala-
tine in 1613, he was not slow in accepting, and even
accompanied her to Heidelburg. Doubtless many a
gay Cavalier would have been contented to spend his
remaining days amidst the overflowing tuns of the
ancient college-town; but evidently the moral
Quarles was of a different nature, for in 1620 we see
him once more in the foggy streets of London.

During the next year — he was not yet twenty-
nine — one of his books, *Hadessa, the History of
Queen Esther,* appeared, and was received with so
much favor as to encourage him to follow it with
such other religious verses as *Sion's Elegies,* in 1624,
Sion's Sonnets, in 1625, and *A Feast of Wormes, set
forth in a Poeme of the Historie of Jonah,* in 1626.
The contents of this last volume were perhaps not
so unsavory as the delectable title would indicate, for
the pious folk of Charles' day seem to have found
considerable delight in the feast. There were, however, in the book other poems that doubtless account
for much of the pleasure; such as *A Hymn to God,*
eleven spiritual meditations, and a collection of devotional verses entitled *Pentelogia, or the Quintes-*

sence of Meditation. When you have read the list of titles in that volume you have gained a very fair idea of what Quarles' life-work was to be — a study of man's relations to the Divine.

In 1625, however, he turned aside for a space to elegiac verse. At this time came his quaint *Alphabet of Elegies upon the Much and Truly Lamented Death of Doctor Aylmer* — twenty-two twelve-line stanzas and a verse epitaph, each line beginning with the requisite letter. How people admired it three centuries ago! This quiet fellow, Francis Quarles, began to cut something of a figure in the literary world. That his popularity had not diminished by 1631 is shown by the fact that his epitaph on Michael Drayton was carved upon the brave old singer's tomb in Westminster. It was this same year that he told, with " many a flirt and flutter," his *History of Samson.* Clearly, Samson was out-Samsoned; but the story suited the taste of the times, and when in 1632 *Divine Fancies, Digested into Epigrams, Meditations, and Observations* appeared, the people were all but ready to crown him king of England's bards. The " people," notice, please; for the literary lights sat about the London coffee-tables and either sneered at his religious effusions or ignored them altogether.

But little cared Francis Quarles for all this. He sat at home with his admiring wife and eighteen children — or those of them who had appeared on the scene at this date — and wrote for that most enduring of audiences, the common folk. Not that

he lacked friends among the London critics and authors. We find that after addressing some verses to
Edward Benlowes he was introduced by the flattered
gentleman to Phineas Fletcher, and lo! the result is
two of Francis Quarles' poems in Fletcher's *Purple
Island,* printed in London in 1633. Moralizing philosopher though he was, he seems always to have had
a keen eye for his earthly prosperity. The court
records show that in 1626 he was prosecuting a London woman for picking his pockets, and during the
same year he was striving in a most businesslike
manner to have Parliament erect works for manu-
facturing salt-petre by a new process. Doubtless,
he was finding that his numerous family could not
subsist on poetical meditations.

Yet it must be confessed that only necessity kept
his mind fixed on earthly things. Almost every contemporary mention of him declares him a man of
genuine piety. In 1629, while he was private secretary to Archbishop Usher of Armagh, and was
living in Dublin, that churchman frequently referred
to him in letters to London friends, and always the
poet was considered as one whose deeds befitted his
songs. 'Again, however, we find that he did not neg-
lect worldly duties for heavenly meditations, since
in 1631 he obtained control of the import duties on
tobacco and pipes brought into Ireland, gaining
thereby no small revenue. It was while in Dublin
that he wrote his first secular poem, *Argalus and
Parthenia* (1629), a story drawn from Sidney's *Arcadia.* It may have appealed to his plainer-spoken

age; but to-day we find in parts of it something that smacks of the indecent. It was, however, but a temporary lapse, and in the eyes of his old-time readers may have been considered none at all.

In all ages men have generally associated meditation with the calm and peace of deep woods and quiet fields. Francis Quarles had thus far " wrought in sad sincerity " amidst the hurly-burly of teeming London or amidst the ancient stench of Dublin; but in 1635 he — quaint old fellow and lover of angling — was back in Essex, and there at Roxwell was finishing that work which was to make his name remembered for centuries — *Emblems Divine and Moral.* How marvelously successful it was! How it was quoted! How men read it from youth to tottering age! Its charms had not vanished even as late as the nineteenth century. Robert Browning declares in one of his letters,[4] " It was my childhood's pet book." But all critics have not been so charitable. Southey disdainfully asserts that only the quaint prints by William Marshall made the book popular; while snappish Pope declares that it is a work

"Where the pictures for the pages atone,
And Quarles is saved by beauties not his own." [5]

It must be admitted that, in a sense not realized by him, the great " Interrogation Point " told the truth about the matter: for, of the five books composing

[4] *Letters,* Vol. II, p. 444.
[5] *Dunciad,* Bk. I, pp. 139, 140.

the volume, the last three are merely translations
and paraphrases of a once noted Jesuit work, *Pia
Desideria Emblematis,* written by Hermann Hugo
and published in Antwerp in 1624. But what of
that? The work was entertaining and pleased the
people, and in the good old days they were not so
particular about the originality of a book.

Fortune was now indeed smiling upon Francis
Quarles. In 1638 another volume of his, *Hieroglyphickes of the Life of Man,* illustrated by Marshall, was welcomed by the common folk and sneered
at by the coffee-house folk, and altogether received
much notice. That same year, too, he was requested
to send out to the lonely colonists in New England
some bits of pious verse, and as a consequence he
gave to John Josselyn, to take to John Cotton and
John Winthrop, metrical versions of six psalms, all
of which appeared in that antique curiosity, *The
Whole Book of Psalms,* published at Boston in 1640.
We have seen that Quarles possessed considerable
business sense, and as he was always exceedingly
shrewd in the dedication of his books his compliments
often brought results of decided material value.
The honor in *Divine Fancies* and *Hieroglyphickes*
had been bestowed upon the wife of the Earl of Dorset, and one morning Quarles awoke to find himself
appointed, through that noble's influence, Chronol-
oger of London. The work was light, the income
was fair, and the poet had leisure to evolve vast numbers of rhyming meditations.

But he failed to do so. Troublous days were at

hand, and, though he wrote some prose essays on
piety he seemed to find little in the time and place
to incite him to song. A sturdy Royalist, he visited Charles I in that year of unrest, 1644, and
published in defense of his king a most zealous
pamphlet, *The Loyal Convert*. There was no
mincing of words with this puritanical Cavalier;
Cromwell was a " professed defacer of churches and
rifler of the monuments of the dead." *The Whipper
Whipt* and *The New Distemper* continued the argument in the same flattering style, and when Cromwell
came into power, doubtless Francis Quarles fancied
that his own day of judgment had arrived. Little
we know of those last days of the poet. Toward
the last, Puritan soldiers searched his library and
destroyed his manuscripts, and a " petition was pre-
ferred against him by eight men." This, it seems,
broke his loyal heart, and he gave up life on September 8th, 1644, having, as his publisher, Royston,
declared, dedicated his all to his king " till death
darkened that great light in his soul." He lies
buried in the church of St. Olave, Silver Street,
London.

The fame of many authors dies with them. That
of Francis Quarles increased for many years after
his death. For more than a century publishers
reaped a bountiful harvest from his field, and the
volumes still found in the humble homes of England
show how wide was the extent of that field. Various
new works continued to appear after their author's
bones had been returned to earth. In 1645 came

Solomon's Recantation, a paraphrase of Ecclesiastes; in 1646 *The Shepherd's Oracles,* dealing with the theological quarrels of the day; and in 1649 *The Virgin Widow,* a play which had been acted privately at Chelsea, and which Langbaine has charitably described as " an innocent, inoffensive play." Thus, year after year works which doubtless he had never hoped to see in print, and never did see, came from the press and sold well.

What was the charm of it all? we of to-day ask in some astonishment. In much of it we can see but the conventional, dull thinking of a devout but uninspired churchman. We find much repetition, no little carelessness in versification, and at times a " bitter melancholy " that sounds false to our more optimistic ears. Just here, however, in this " artificial " sadness, is the secret of much of Quarles' success; a poetic melancholy was extremely popular in Cavalier days. According to their own verses, many of the knights of the time were about to expire for the sake of their lady-loves; we find frank, gay-hearted Sir John Suckling considered something of a wonder because of his refusal to die in this manner; we hear men sounding the same artificial note in their religious poetry. Doubtless, Francis Quarles did not consider his note at any time false, for he was a sincere man; but, leaving out of consideration the day and its tastes, and viewing his meditations with the eyes of common sense, we of this century feel that his notions of life and its attendant evils were most extravagant. Unceasingly he seems

to be crying: "O wretched man that I am, who shall
deliver me from the body of this death?"

> "And what's a life,—a weary pilgrimage,
>   When glory in one day doth fill the stage
>   With childhood, manhood, and decrepit age." [6]

Doubtless the Puritan faith was beginning to
cause men, even Cavaliers, to question more earnestly
the vanities, the beauties, aye, the very comforts of
this earthly existence, and this but aided in the tendency toward a wider separation of the aesthetic and
the ethical. How Herrick's soul longed for the
aesthetic, and how Quarles' embraced the ethical!
Life and its lovely things were earthly, and were
they not, therefore, sinful?   Sing of God, concludes
Quarles—God and his relations to our soul; these
are the only worthy themes.   Thus our Cavalier
singer became what Professor Schelling calls a " devotional pamphleteer," [7] and long remained the
most popular of the numerous tribe which soon
sprang into existence.   And by the false standards
of the day devoutness meant crying aloud, " Vanity,
all is vanity!"

> " Can he be fair, that withers at a blast?
>   Or he be strong, that airy breath can cast?" [8]

How he parades the ethical purpose! But a
poet must sing to his age or else fail, and the innu-

[6] *The Shortness of Life.*
[7] *Seventeenth Century Lyrics,* p. 47.
[8] *Mors Tua.*

merable editions of Quarles' religious verse declare
that he must have satisfied a longing in thousands
and thousands of simple, trusting hearts. Dull he
may seem to us at this late hour; didactic he undoubtedly was; but, after all, if he bound up the
broken heart and dried the penitent's tears, he
served his age as every poet should. Surely his
songs were not written in vain.

" To heaven's high city I direct my journey,
  Whose spangled suburbs entertain mine eye;
  Mine eye, by contemplation's great attorney,
  Transcends the crystal pavement of the sky:
  But what is heaven, great God, compared to thee!
  Without thy presence, heaven's no heaven to me." [9]

We may well believe Phillips, who, writing in
1675, declared that Quarles' poems " have been ever,
and still are, in wonderful veneration among the vul-
gar," [10] and condemn at the same time Anthony à
Wood's sneering remark that he was " the some-
time darling of our plebeian judgment." The poet
must sing not to the college professor, but to the
people; else he will never have the precious honor of
being discussed by the said professor! The common folk are the surest guardians of poetry, and
Quarles appealed directly to them. Those average
readers of the seventeenth century believed in a
wrathful God, and consequently they admired the
rigor of such lines as those found in *O Whither Shall
I Fly:*

9 *Delight in God.*
10 *Theatrum Poetarum.*

" O whither shall I fly? what path untrod
Shall I seek out to 'scape the flaming rod
Of my offended, of my angry God? "

The religious readers of the century believed, too,
in a stern repression of self; for passions, appetites,
mere desires, were of the devil. The stern note of
Oliver's dauntless Ironsides may be heard already in
Quarles' poem, *Faith:*

" But wouldst thou conquer, have thy conquest crown'd
By hands of Seraphims, triumph'd with the sound
Of heaven's loud trumpet, warbled by the shrill
Celestial choir, recorded with a quill
Pluck'd from the pinion of an angel's wing,
Confirmed with joy by heaven's eternal King;
Conquer thyself."

" Some poets," says blunt, old-fashioned Thomas
Fuller, " if debarred profaneness, wantonness, and
satyricalness (that they may neither abuse God,
themselves, nor their neighbors) have their tongues
cut out in effect. Others only trade in wit at the
second-hand, being all for translations, nothing for
invention. Our Quarles was free from the faults
of the first, as if he had drank[*sic*] of Jordan instead of Helicon, and slept on Mount Olivet for his
Parnassus; and was happy in his own invention." [11]
All very well, friend Fuller; but this more critical
day demands the reason for certain blemishes which
doubtless you never considered worthy of notice.

[11] *Worthies of England.*

Like all other singers in the metaphysical choir,
Francis Quarles was entirely too profuse with figures. What shifting of similes and metaphors in
his love-song, *My beloved is Mine and I Am His!*
The first stanza declares the lovers to be

" Ev'n like the two little bank-dividing brooks,
    [That wash the pebbles with their wanton streams; "

In the second stanza she has turned to flax and
he to a consuming flame. In the fifth she exclaims:

" He's mine by water, I am his by wine; "

and in the sixth she declares:

" He's my supporting elm and I his vine."

And yet, in spite of the incongruous mixture, grace
and beauty are not absent.

This constant striving for rhetorical surprises,
this discovering of likenesses where likenesses never
existed, this indiscriminate loquacity on every subject, this carelessness of comparison and figure,
caused by too intense gazing at the subject — these
come near to destroying Quarles' chance for lasting
fame. Yet one must feel that here is real and sincere emotion. The songster is flying hard; now and
then he hits the ground with a ridiculous flop; but,
after all, his aim is high and he soars at times.
There is many a notable thought amidst this mass
of commonplace. " Subdue thyself; thyself's a

world to thee." " Hath Heaven despoil'd what his
full hand hath given thee?" " Heaven holds not
out His bow for ever bent.":

> " May not a potter that from out the ground
> Hath framed a vessel, search if it be sound? "

And are there not in these lines from an elegy on one
of his friends the characteristics of good poetry?

> " No azure dapples my be-darkened skies;
> My passion has no April in her eyes."

No, Francis Quarles has hardly received fair treatment from disgruntled old Time. An originality of
images, a multitude of noble thoughts, a splendid
use of language, cannot be denied him. At times
he is too fanciful; at times he is obscure; but never
is he without spirit and a certain rough vigor, a real
knowledge of human nature and its needs, a moral
uplift born of his earnest efforts to relieve those
needs. Perhaps, after all, the man was capable of
greater work, but was limited by the tastes of the
day — tastes which compelled him to " turn out copy
to order," tastes which made him what Saintsbury
calls " a journalist in verse." " I should not like,"
continues this most artistic critic of these later days,
" to be challenged to produce twenty good lines of
his in verse or prose written consecutively, yet it
might be a still more dangerous challenge to produce
any journalist in verse or prose of the present day
who has written so much, and in whom the occasional

flashes — the signs of poetical power in the individual and of what may be called poetical atmosphere in his surroundings — are more frequent." [12]

With these kind words let us cease from inquiry into the life and verses of Francis Quarles. Times limit men's visions. He could not quite see the greater mysteries with Shakespeare; he could not hear them with Tennyson. His age in its conventional religious moods looked upon earth as a slough of despond, and he knew only how to sing accordingly.

> " What well-advised ear regards
>   What earth can say?
> Thy words are gold, but thy rewards
>   Are painted clay.
> Thy cunning can but pack the cards,
>   Thou canst not play." [13]

[12] *History of Elizabethan Literature*, p. 378.
[13] *The Vanity of the World.*

GEORGE HERBERT

(1593 — 1633)

Wise and simple-hearted King Alfred once said that we all love the reputation of being Christians, but do not love the necessary deeds. Men prate much of the Golden Rule, but prefer to use the iron one. There once lived in Cavalier days a saintly poet who prated little and practised much, and daily bore his cross of sacrifice with a meekness that turned scoffers into worshippers. His name was George Herbert. " That man's life," says Hutton, " was itself the noblest of his poems, and while it had the beauty of his verses, it had their quaintness, as well." [1]

Go, look at the face of this pious singer, with its strange mingling of strength and weakness, manliness and effeminacy, triumph and anguish — that long but not unhandsome countenance, the steeple forehead, a nose and a chin with a slight hint of puritanical sharpness about them, a dainty, wee bit of mustache, a fine, eager, gentle mouth, a pair of steady, thoughtful eyes, with deepening lines between them and about the nostrils. Here is an intense soul that has suffered — ah, suffered vastly. Many have remarked on that countenance. " His

[1] *Social England,* Vol. IV, p. 34.

face is the face of a spirit dimly bright," writes
Mrs. Browning,[2] while Alexander Grosart, zealous
scholar and keen observer, notes the " thought-lined
burdened-eyed, translucent as if transfigured face.
. . . There is a noble ' ivory palace ' for the meek
and holy soul there; brow steep rather than wide; lips
tremulous as with music; nose pronounced as Richard Baxter's; cheeks worn and thin; hair full and
flowing as in younger days: altogether, a face which
one could scarcely pass without note — all the more
that there are lines in it which inevitably suggest
that if George Herbert mellowed into the sweet lov-
ingness and gentleness of John ' whom Jesus loved,'
it was of grace and through masterdom of a naturally lofty, fiery spirit." [3]   And quaint old Izaak
Walton, who walked among men with a shrewd but
ever kindly disposed soul, looked upon him with love,
and wrote: " His aspect was cheerful, and his
speech and motion did both declare him a gentleman;
for they were all so meek and obliging that they purchased love and respect from all that knew him." [4]
And listen: " Some of the meaner sort of his parish
did so love and reverence Mr. Herbert that they
would let their plough rest when Mr. Herbert's
Saint's bell rung to prayers; that they might also
offer their devotions to God with him; and would
then return back to their plough.   And his most
holy life was such that it begot such reverence to

2 *The Book of the Poets*, Vol. II, p. 5.
3 *Leisure Hours*, Vol. XXII, p. 455.
4 *Life of George Herbert.*

God and to him that they thought themselves the happier when they carried Mr. Herbert's blessing back with them to their labor. Thus powerful was his reason and example to persuade others to a practical piety and devotion." [5]

What an opportunity for an artist! — the plowman bowing in the lonely field while within the distant church the beloved priest calls upon their common God. Such a man, then, was the author of *The Temple*. In that short life of forty years there was a soul-battle full of merciless anguish — a soul-battle waged from the gaudiest temple of world-pride to the white steps of Heaven itself.

In the proud days before Cromwell there stood near Montgomery, Wales, an ancient castle where many a gay and brilliant courtier had lived and loved and reveled and gone forth to battle for his king. That home no longer stands, for the stormy days of the Commonwealth saw it fall into ruin. But here in the old days the Herberts had dwelt, and had pointed with pride to the long line of knights that led back to the brave Earl of Pembroke, in the time of King Edward IV. Here the poet, George Herbert, was born in 1593, a younger son in a family of ten children. The old-fashioned family grew to a most estimable manhood and womanhood, and one son besides George brought fresh fame to the name — the talented and somewhat erratic Lord Herbert of Cherbury. The father died when the future poet was a child of four, leaving the little ones to the

[5] Walton, *Life of George Herbert*.

care of their beautiful, brilliant, lovable, but undoubtedly imperious mother. In admiration of her intellectual strength Dr. Donne, a founder of the metaphysical school, wrote:

> " In all her words to every hearer fit,
> You may at revels or at council sit."

She it was who first directed his mind toward that intense regard for religion which, increasing with the years, at length changed his soul into a living sacrifice for things divine.

Under her guidance he laid the foundation of his thorough education and entered Westminster School exceptionally well prepared. It has been said that pride of family made him somewhat reserved toward the other boys there; but hear once more the words of quiet-voiced Walton: " The beauties of his pretty behavior and wit shined and became so eminent and lovely in this his innocent age that he seemed to be marked out for piety and to become the care of Heaven and of a particular good angel to guard and guide him." [6]   He entered Trinity in 1609, was a B. A. in 1611, was elected a fellow of Trinity in 1614, and received his M. A. in 1615. His career as a university man was nothing short of brilliant. He was chosen Public Orator of the University in 1619 and held the position for eight years. He counted among his intimate friends such men as Sir Henry Wotton, the Duke of Richmond, the Marquis

[6] *Life of George Herbert.*

of Hamilton and the famous Dr. Donne. Even
Lord Bacon had this youth look over his philosophical works, and meekly, indeed, the great philosopher
received the young man's criticisms. One day the
ambitious orator wrote a Latin letter to the king,
thanking him for a book, and so exquisitely formed
was the Latin that the ruler declared him the jewel
of the University. Excellent student that he was,
however, he was still a gay and worldly fellow. He
seldom attended to the duties of his oratorship unless the king himself was to be present; but on such
occasions he delivered addresses so brilliant and so
skilfully phrased that his royal audience went away
enthusiastic. And his reward was not slow to follow: we find the sovereign giving him an office which
required not one whit of labor save drawing one hundred and twenty pounds a year. " With this money,"
writes Walton, " and his annuity and the advantages
of his college and of his oratorship, he enjoyed his
genteel humor for clothes and court-like company,
and seldom looked toward Cambridge . . . " 7
Thus, at twenty-six, his course through life seemed
assured of smoothness, pleasure, and idleness.

At length, however, there came into his life, as
into every man's, a crisis, a turning-point where his
decision meant either success or destruction. For
several years Herbert had been hoping, and with good
reason, for high office in the government service.
His influential friends and the king's outspoken admiration entirely warranted such expectations. But

7 *Life of George Herbert.*

King James passed away, and so did other friends, and Herbert, hopeless of advancement in secular office, turned to that institution for which he was so admirably fitted — the Church. The unfeigned devoutness of the man was remarkable. Searching among his effects after his death, his friends came across an engraved figure of the Christ crucified on an anchor — the image a parting gift of Dr. Donne's — and upon it the saintly Herbert had written:

"When my dear friend could write no more,
He gave this seal and so gave o'er.

"When winds and waves rise highest, I am sure
This anchor keeps my faith, that me, secure."

For a little time before entering his new sphere of life he lived in almost complete solitude at a friend's house in Kent. He feared to undertake the work of a priest; strange to say, he did not consider himself good enough! In July, 1626, he was given as his charge Leyton Ecclesia, a village in Huntingdon — and what a charge it was! The church was in so dilapidated a condition that it had not been used for twenty years; there was no home for the clergyman, and the people had seemingly lost all spiritual ambition. Undismayed, however, the inexperienced Herbert entered the field, begged contributions from relatives and friends far and near, and soon built one of the most artistic small churches in all England. Still he hesitated to become a regularly ordained minister of the Church of England. The constant question before him seems to have been: "Will my soul stand the test?" But zealous Nicholas Ferrar and that mighty worker, Laud, were numbered among his friends, and they so placed the matter before him that he was induced to take holy orders in 1630. He seemed to be blindly following what he considered God's will, for hear what he wrote in *Affliction*, soon after becoming a rector:

"Now I am here, what Thou wilt do with me
None of my books will show;
I read, and sigh, and wish I were a tree;
For then sure should I grow
To fruit or shade; at least some bird would trust
Her household to me, and I should be just."

A miserably poor comparison, perhaps; but it shows, at least, the utter trustfulness and real desire of the man.

The remainder of Herbert's life was to be spent at Bemerton, in Wiltshire. Like most sensible men, he very soon reached the conclusion that life as a bachelor was not the ideal state of man, and he married his wife the third day after meeting her. This was, indeed, short work; but Izaak Walton declares that the girl's father had so praised the gentle poet and preacher that she was in love with him before they ever met. And listen to the quaint old fisher's account of their honeymoon experience: "The third day after he was made rector of Bemerton and had changed his sword and silk clothes into a canonical habit, he returned so habited . . . to Bemerton; and immediately after he had seen and saluted his wife, he said to her: ' You are now a minister's wife, and must now so far forget your father's house as not to claim a precedence of any of your parishioners; for you are to know that a priest's wife can challenge no precedence or place but that which she purchases by her obliging humility; and I am sure places so purchased do best become them.' " [8]   And Walton says the bride cheerfully acquiesced, and from that day was almost as noted for her meekness, constant sacrifice, and charities as was her husband.

There is a modern evangelist who holds that the clergyman of to-day is preaching the Reverend John Smith and him dignified instead of Jesus Christ and Him crucified.   Not so with George Herbert.   His first sermon at Bemerton was a brilliant exposition, full of learning and ornament,— just to show them that he could — but at the close of it he meekly announced to his hearers that " his language and his expressions should be more plain and practical in his future sermons," as he did not wish to " fill their heads with unnecessary notions." [9]   Then, too, look some time through his little book, *The Country Parson*.   He set himself to the task of making these rules, not for the guidance of others but for himself; and yet, as Izaak Walton has said, the preacher " that can spare twelve pence and yet wants it [the book] is scarce excusable." [10]

Life to such a man could not be a long day of lux-

[8] *Life of George Herbert.*
[9] Walton, *Life of George Herbert.*
[10] Walton, *Life of George Herbert.*

urious ease; it meant an unceasing struggle with the
powers of evil.   But the good wife stood beside him,
and then, too, he had his music for consolation.   And
how he loved music!   He once exclaimed that it
" raised his weary soul so far above the earth that
it gave him an earnest of the joys of heaven before
he possessed them." [11]   He was a capital hand at
the lute, and was accustomed to set his own sacred
verses to music and to sing them of evenings.   The
scene brings to mind another struggler, Martin Lu-
ther, who in his hours of utter weariness and despair
turned to the viol and song for consolation, and came
back to the world refreshed and strengthened.

George Herbert must have been indeed a lovable
man.   So many little acts of his life testify to that
singular sincerity which made men wonder, admire,
and love.   When, according to the ancient custom,
he entered alone into the church to pray and to toll
the bell announcing a new rector, he stayed within
so much longer than was expected that his friends,
in alarm, crept to a window and looked in.   And
there, lying prostrate before the altar, he was found
praying and vowing undying allegiance to the duties
of his new office.   Widely, too, the story was told of
how an old woman, coming before him to speak of her
sorrows, was so overcome by the majesty and noble-
ness of his face that she could not speak; how he
took her by the hand, reassured her, and, after lis-
tening patiently to her story, sent her home with a
cheerful heart, praising God and praying for the

[11] Walton, *Life of George Herbert.*

good pastor. Then, too, all the country round had
heard that, as he was walking to Salisbury to attend
a meeting of his beloved music club, he met a poor
fellow driving a worn-out nag, staggering under its
load, and that, throwing off his clergyman's coat,
he helped unload the animal. When he appeared,
sweaty and dirty, at the meeting of the club, what
an answer was that which he gave to a disgusted
member: "If I be bound to pray for all that be in
distress, I am sure that I am bound to practise what
I pray for." Again, as he went along that same
ancient Salisbury road, meeting a country gentleman, he asked him about his faith, and so gently and
so meekly advised him that the man fell in love with
the unknown clergyman, and often went out of his
way to meet the sweet-faced follower of Christ. He
lived as he taught. Every morning and every evening he went with his little family into the church
and read the service; a tenth part of his total income he gave to his wife to distribute to the poor;
he lived to serve. After building his Bemerton
home at his own expense and with much actual labor
on his own part, he asked but one thing of his suc-
cessors, and this request he engraved on the fire-
place:

> " *To My Successor.*
> " If thou chance to find
> A new home to thy mind,
>   And built without thy cost;
> Be good to the poor
> As God gives thee store,
>   And then my labour's not lost."

Thus he went in and out among men — an exemplar for all his humble parishoners.

But now came the last struggle. For some years he had been threatened with consumption, and in 1631 he began to show alarming signs of a decline. He labored on, however, hoping doubtless to forget his disease in his work, but at length became too feeble to read the church service. He knew that now at last Death stood beside him. Those last few days were full of pathetic incidents. The Sunday before his death he rose suddenly from his couch, called for his music, and sang his own once well-known lyric:

> " The Sundays of man's life,
>   Threaded together on Time's string,
>   Make bracelets to adorn the wife
>   Of the eternal glorious King."

As the last hour approached, his friend, Mr. Duncan, visited him. The dying Herbert brought forth a manuscript volume of poems, handed it to the visitor, and " with a thoughtful and contented look " said to him: " Sir, I pray deliver this little book to my dear brother Ferrar, and tell him he shall find in it a picture of the many spiritual conflicts that have passed betwixt God and my soul, before I could subject mine to the will of Jesus my Master; in whose service I have now found perfect freedom; desire him to read it; and then, if he can think it may turn to the advantage of any dejected poor soul, let it be made public; if not, let him burn it, for I and it are less than the least of God's mercies." [12] And thus

[12] Walton, *Life of George Herbert.*

he passed on, breathing the simple prayer, "Lord, now receive my soul." "He was buryed (according to his own desire)," says John Aubrey, "with the singing services for the buriall of dead by the singing men of Sarum." He sleeps at Bemerton, and as one walks out from Salisbury one may see among the trees in the distance the beautiful church erected to his memory.

"Sir, I pray deliver this little book." The little book was the famous *Temple, or Sacred Poems and Private Ejaculations,* a quaint collection that has been bread and wine to many a weary and hungry soul. We of this age, somewhat indifferent as to modes and regularity of worship, find little of the food which other generations discovered; perhaps, however, that is our fault and not the book's. To us it is "a quaint and curious volume of forgotten lore," and its expressions seem at times even grotesque. And, true enough, its figures of speech and carefully involved phrases are eccentric. But this trait has perhaps been over-emphasized. Gosse speaks of his "excessive pseudo-psychological ingenuity"; Whipple calls his verse a "*bizarre* expression"; and James Montgomery declares that it is "devotion turned into masquerade"; but a close study of his phrases will lead one to believe, with Craik, that the quaintness lies in his thoughts rather than in their expression, "which is in general sufficiently simple and luminous." [13]

It must be admitted, however, that there are too

[13] *Compendious History of English Literature,* Vol. II, p. 19.

many riddles, too many oddities, too many fantastic fancies. Religion had become so familiar to him that he dallied and toyed with it. Too often the page is blemished with such a conceit as

" God gave thy soul brave wings; put not those feathers
Into a bed to sleep out all ill weathers."

And yet it requires something of an inventive mind to create such webs of unsuspected relationships and comparisons. Certainly he was original; certainly he was imaginative; certainly in another day, through these gifts, he might have produced beautiful structures; but the style of his age turned his thoughts into the alien channel of the far-fetched and over-quaint, and his talents failed to bring forth their highest possibilities. His rhythms are often intricate, and even the very forms of some of his most heartfelt poems are fantastic. Note, in *Easter Wings*, how the verses fall into the outlines of wings, how the lines diminish as his pride diminishes, how they increase as his confidence in God increases:

" Lord, who createdst man in wealth and store,
Though foolishly he lost the same,
Decaying more and more
Till he became
Most poor:

" With thee
O let me rise,
As larks, harmoniously,
And sing this day thy victories:
Then shall the fall further the flight in me."

The day demanded poetic wings and altars and crosses, and so did succeeding days, until Dryden ridiculed the whole matter in *Mac Flecknoe:*

> " Choose for thy command
> Some peaceful province in acrostic land,
> Where thou may'st *wings* display or *altars* raise,
> And torture one poor word ten thousand ways."

Think what we may about these eccentricities, we must see that Herbert long filled a need. Sincere man that he was, religious by nature, and born to be thoughtful, his simple-minded and single-minded devoutness encouraged and inspired many a flagging soul, and led men to believe, with Richard Baxter, that " heart-work and heaven-work make up his books." [14] To this day critics may come to scoff in Herbert's *Temple;* but they are more than likely to remain to pray. Many a reader would echo the sentiment of free-thinking Samuel Coleridge, who, writing in 1818, declared: " I find more substantial comfort now in pious George Herbert's *Temple,* which I used to read to amuse myself with his quaintness, in short, only to laugh at, than in all the poetry since the poems of Walton." [15] Cowley, Quarles, Crashaw, and other religious song-writers of the era may have been more brilliant and far more accurate in thought and in composition; but here is an intense earnestness, a clutching at the things eternal, a desperate battling, which is alien to his

[14] *Poetical Fragments.*
[15] *Lectures and Notes on Shakespeare.*

fellow-singers. Read his *Lines on Man,* " one of the profoundest utterances of the Elizabethan age," according to Whipple,[16] or note in *Frailty* the psalm-like vigor and directness when his soul rises to its full vision of the world's temptations.

Soul-earnestness goes a long way in art and will cover a multitude of technical sins. In spite of the confusion of comparisons, the illogical mingling of figures, these outpourings from the heart of Herbert tell, and tell effectively, of suffering and tears and patient waiting; and be they artistic or crude, they flow on into the hearts of other men. Read the last lines of *Employment,* and confess that, in their sad sincerity and simplicity of mood, they must be classed among the beautiful prayers of man.

Perhaps the reason of Herbert's success lies in the fact that every one loves to study the development of a human soul. Here in *The Temple* we find just such an aspiring soul as all men, good or wicked, admire — a soul struggling to assert itself and to claim mastery over the temptations of a most tempting age. To such a spirit the warfare never can be mild. What a feverish anxiety is in his inward glance! What positive terror at times! The lyric confidence of that glad-hearted devotee, Crashaw, is impossible to him; he can but cry for mercy. His was a mind of naturally great possibilities, and, active enterprises for these being denied, that hungry mind began to feed upon itself. Therefore, in spite of the declaration that " as a manual of devo-

[16] *Literature of the Age of Elizabeth,* p. 248.

tion, it is as though a seraph covered his face with his wings in rapturous adoration," [17] in spite of Emerson's belief that " so much piety was never married to so much wit," [18] in spite of Ferrar's claim that there is " a picture of a divine soul in every page," it must be admitted that these songs of Herbert's pain-wrung heart are coldly puritanical when compared to the rich, gorgeous, cathedral tone of Crashaw's chants.   But here in Herbert is a psychological insight far beyond the scope of his lyrical contemporary.   Here is something Browning-like in the keen observation of critical moments in soulgrowth.   He had suffered as other men had suffered; he had felt the blush of humiliation and the pangs of remorse; and he could picture with appealing and effective realism the conflicts of spirit and earth.

The best poetry of the man came in those two years of keenest anguish when he was hesitating between the world and the Church; and perhaps this is the reason that he betrays a conscience morbid and almost diseased in its tenderness.   His is a stern, Puritan view of the vanity of all earthly things:

> " Lord, in my silence how do I despise
>   What upon trust
> Is styled honor, riches, or fair eyes,
>   But is fair dust!"

And yet he is not without tenderness.   How many a heart his little poem *Virtue* has consoled!

[17] John Brown, "The Parson of Bemerton," *Good Words*, Vol. XXXI, p. 697.
[18] *Parnassus*, Preface.

" Only a sweet and virtuous soul,
   Like seasoned timber, never gives;
But though the whole world turn to coal,
   Then chiefly lives."

The volume is, indeed, " a book in which by declaring his own spiritual conflicts he hath comforted and raised many a dejected and discomposed soul, and charmed them into sweet and quiet thoughts; a book, by the frequent reading whereof, and the assistance of that spirit that seemed to inspire the Author, the Reader may attain habits of Peace and Piety, and all the gifts of the Holy Ghost and Heaven; and may, by still reading, still keep those sacred fires burning upon the altar of so pure a heart, as shall free it from the anxieties of this world, and keep it fixed upon things that are above." [19]

Will this poet of prayers and tears and trust live? Probably his fame is secure. In its own day *The Temple* was in every cultured home. By 1674 twenty thousand copies had been sold, and Cowley was the only clerical poet who could rival him in popularity. Among the more strictly orthodox of modern English and American readers he undoubtedly holds his own; and that is saying much for a minor poet. And who can tell what change may come? At times there sweep over all nations mighty waves of religious enthusiasm, and at such times the half-neglected thinkers and singers of past days are frequently brought forth to speak once more. Whether or not such fortune will ever fall to this poet cannot

[19] Walton, *Life of Dr. John Donne.*

be known; but this much is certain: " Myriads treasure in their heart of hearts the poems of George Herbert who know little and do not care to know more of the mighty sons of song." [20]

[20] Grosart, *Leisure Hours,* Vol. XXII, p. 325.

THOMAS CAREW

(1598 — 1639)

Sir John Suckling, who seemed to believe poetry the easy offspring of inspiration, once expressed himself concerning Carew in these words:

> " Tom Carew was next, but he had a fault
> That would not well stand with a laureat;
> His muse was hide-bound, and the issue of 's brain
> Was seldom brought forth but with trouble and pain.

> " All that were present there did agree,
> A laureate muse should be easy and free,
> Yet sure 'twas not that, but 'twas thought that his
>   grace
> Considered he was well he had a cup-bearer's place." [1]

There is an old belief, however, that hard writing makes easy reading, and Tom Carew's poems, especially his lyrics, so concealed the " trouble and pain " of their birth that they were more in demand than the verses of any other poet of the day. Anthony à Wood, the seventeenth-century chronicler, tells how the English folk were pleased with " the charming sweetness of his lyric odes and amorous sonnets "; [2] those quaint composers, William and

[1] *Sessions of the Poets.*
[2] *Athenae Oxonienses,* Vol. I, p. 630.

Henry Lawes, delighted to put his songs to music; while the king himself did not disdain to act a part in that heavy but gorgeous masque, *Caelum Britannicum*, performed at Whitehall in 1633, with Henry Lawes in charge of the fiddlers and Inigo Jones shifting the scenes. The king admired his somewhat indolent but poetically conscientious singer, feasted him into fatness, and in a not unusual burst of liberality gave him the royal domain of Sunningshill, in Windsor Forest.

What manner of man was this who held the friendship of king and courtiers and lost it not? Izaak Walton, who knew him, declared him " a great libertine in his life and talke ";[3] Anthony à Wood said of him, " He became reckon'd among the chiefest of his time for delicacy of wit and poetic fancy ";[4] while his personal friend, Lord Clarendon, wrote in later days, " Carew was a person of a pleasant and facetious wit and made many poems (especially in the amorous way) which, for the sharpness of the fancy and the elegance of the language in which that fancy was spread, were at least equal, if not superior, to any of that time."[5] Carew had ample time, indeed, to air that " pleasant and facetious wit," for life was for him but a path of roses — of the hothouse variety.

Born in London, the son of a favorite and highly respectable knight, Sir Matthew Carew, Master in

[3] *Fulman MSS.* See *Notes and Queries,* Second Series, Vol. VI, p. 12.
[4] *Athenae Oxonienses,* Vol. I, p. 630.
[5] Clarendon, *Life,* p. 9.

Chancery, the boy attended Corpus Christi College, Oxford, read much that was not in the curriculum, and very little that was in it, and left without his degree. The old father worried over the son's wild habits — the same habits, doubtless, that the father himself had followed in his youth in Shakespeare's merry London — and wrote to a friend, Sir Dudley Carleton, that Thomas had been sent to the Middle Temple to study law but was doing little. Carleton generously offered to make the young scapegrace his secretary, and in this capacity took him to Venice and Turin. But in 1615 young Tom Carew had returned to England; even a secretaryship to a knight was too arduous an occupation for him. The gray-haired father, in despair over the black sheep in his eminently conservative and respected flock, now turned to another son, the gallant Sir Matthew, Jr., to uphold the ancient glory of the family. Could he but have looked into the distant future! "While the lives and fortunes of the high judicial functionary and the brave young knight-banneret are forgotten, while the persons of rank, fashion, and influence with whom they mixed have passed, for the most part, completely away, and while even Sir Dudley Carleton is familiar only to a few antiquaries, the lustre which one man of genius has shed on the name of Carew remains unfaded, and can never decline." [6]

In spite of the father's fears Fortune smiled upon the young rascal, and in 1619 we find him bowing his handsome head in the French court, in company

[6] W. C. Hazlitt, ed. *Poems of Carew*, p. 18.

with the accomplished Lord Herbert of Cherbury.
Then came his appointment, " for his most admirable
ingenuity," [7] Gentleman of the Privy Chamber and
Sewer in Ordinary to His Majesty, Charles I, and he
feasted and danced, and presented the admiring ladies with gallant compliments and pretty lyrics, and
grew prematurely old from too much leisure, wine,
and sin, and so ended in his fiftieth year. Lord
Clarendon, who, as has been noted, was his personal
friend, says of that ending: " His glory was that
after fifty years of his life spent with less severity
or exactness than it ought to have been he died with
the greatest manifestations of Christianity that his
best friends could desire." [8] But Isaak Walton
tells a different and a darker story of that passing
out of a poet's soul. Robert Burns once said that a
man might live like a fool, but he scarce died like
one; and so, according to Walton, it was with Carew.
Seized with an extreme illness, he " sent for Mr.
Hales to come to him, . . . and desired his advice and absolution, which Mr. Hales, upon a promise
of amendment, gave him . . . But Mr. Cary
[Carew] came to London, fell to his old company,
and into a more visible scandalous life, and especially
in his discourse, and he being taken very sick, that
which proved his last, and being much troubled in
mind, procured Mr. Hales to come to him in this his
sickness and agony of minde, desyring earnestly,
after a confession of many of his sins, to have his

[7] Wood, *Athenae Oxonienses,* Vol. I, p. 630.
[8] *Life,* p. 9.

prayers and his absolution. Mr. Hales told him he should have his prayers, but would by noe means give him then neither the sacrament or absolution." [9]

As was his life so is his poetry. "He loved wine, and roses, and fair, florid women, to whom he could indite joyous or pensive poems about their beauty, adoring it while it lasted, regretting it when it faded." [10] From such a man we must not expect the mountain-majesty of a Milton or the soul-insight of a Browning. He reaches no great heights of genius; but, on the other hand, he reaches no great depths of mediocrity. Throughout the fragile texture of his songs he sustains a pretty high level; for though in almost every poem the microscopic critic may find at least one ill-expressed phrase, if the critic will cast aside his microscope and view the work with sympathetic human eyes, he will find each lyric not mere disconnected lines of beauty, but a well-woven entirety, an organic whole. One example will suffice — the well-expressed comparison in *The Marigold*:

> "Mark how the bashful morn, in vain,
>   Courts the amorous marigold
> With sighing blasts and weeping rain;
>   Yet she refuses to unfold.
> But when the planet of the day
> Approacheth with his powerful ray,
> Then she spreads, then she receives
> His warmer beams into her virgin leaves.

[9] Walton, *Fulman MSS.* See *Notes and Queries,* **Second** Series, Vol. VI, p. 12.
[10] Ward's *English Poets,* Vol. II, p. 112.

" So shalt thou thrive in love, fond boy;
    If thy tears and sighs discover
Thy grief, thou never shall enjoy
    The just reward of a bold lover.
But when, with moving accents, thou
Shalt constant faith and service vow,
Thy Celia shalt receive those charms
With open ears and with unfolded arms."

Undoubtedly this poet approached mastery in the particular field that he chose to occupy. He wielded English phrases with admirable, even if conscious, ability; he possessed " a command of the overlapped heroic couplet which for sweep and rush of rhythm cannot be surpassed anywhere " ; [11] he almost gave a certain formula to the courtly love poetry of England; he nurtured, if he did not beget, British *vers de société;* and, according to that careful critic, Edmund Gosse, he was " surpassed in genius by Herrick only." [12]   True, his faults are not a few.   His shepherdesses dress in lace and silk.   He knew little of rustic life, and loved brilliancy rather than the freshness of full-blooded open-air life.   He lacked boldness of idea and was content to sing again the conventional sentiments on love's charms, disdainful ladies, and broken hearts.   Then, too, his conceits, under the control of reason though they are, and not to be compared in pedantry to Waller's, are bad enough.   The surgeon bleeding Celia is reminded that the blood he draws comes not from the fair dam-

[11] Saintsbury, *History of Elizabethan Literature,* p. 360.
[12] Ward's *English Poets,* Vol. II, p. 111.

sel's arm but *from her lover's heart.* His cruel mistress he scolds most extravagantly:

> " We read of kings and gods that kindly took
> A pitcher filled with water from the brook;
> But I have daily tendered without thanks
> *Rivers of tears that overflow their banks.*"

All this, however, but made him one of the most
successful court poets of his day. He was so sure
of his audience — that audience of belaced and bepowdered gallants and fair ladies. He knew their
love of fancy and hatred of much thought; he knew
how to soften the hard hearts of each bejeweled Cloe
and Celia. It is no wonder that the indolent fellow
was so conventional; why be otherwise when it brings
all that indolence desires? Indolent he undoubtedly
was, but yet he was a watchful suitor and at times
an ardent singer, one who knew just what rose-leaf
falling on the scales of love and indifference might
win for him victory or disdain. Doubtless he spoke
truly when he declared:

> " Give me a storm; if it be love,
> Like Danaë in that golden shower
> I swim in pleasure."

But there is little of storming in his lines; he wins
by smiles and happy phrases and melodious words.
Masson is right in saying of these olden love lyrics:
" There is a light French spirit in his love poems, a
grace and even a tenderness of sentiment, and a lucid
softness of style, that make them peculiarly pleasing,

and that, even when he becomes licentious, help to save him." [13]

Like Herrick and Suckling and the others, he sang of the conventional spring and maidens, the brevity of life and its sweets, the charms of sensual love, and was concerned altogether with earthly enjoyments. That was what his age wanted, and little he cared for the future's opinion. But, note,— there is a distinction to be made. He lifted his voice, not in the careless, happy-go-lucky way of many of his companions, but with a grace, a polished ease, a nicety of expression that have affected, consciously or unconsciously, all succeeding singers. Others sang fervently; others sang melodiously; but few sang with the same careful art. Critics have not given Tom Carew his full share of credit in that change of taste which resulted in the brilliancy and cold but admirable art of the " classical " school. Long ago, in 1787, the English scholar, Henry Headley, praised this " man of sense, gallantry, and breeding," [14] for the important part he had borne in the quiet but certain revolution from slipshod verse to tight-laced couplets, and Headley's words are worth the attention of students to-day: " Though love," says he, " had long before softened us into civility, yet it was of a formal, ostentatious and romantic cast; and, with very few exceptions, its effects on composition were similar to those on manners. Something more light, unaffected and alluring was still wanting; in

---

[13] *Life of Milton*, Vol. I, ch. vi.
[14] *Select Beauties of Ancient English Poetry*, Vol. I.

everything but sincerity of intention it was deficient.
. . . Carew and Waller jointly began to remedy
these defects. In them Gallantry for the first time
was accompanied by the Graces." [15] The days of
trimness were approaching; hear it in *Persuasions to
Love:*

> " Nor let the brittle beauty make
> You your wiser thoughts forsake:
> For that lovely face will fail,
> Beauty's sweet, but beauty's frail;
> 'Tis sooner past, 'tis sooner done
> Than summer's rain or winter's sun;
> Most fleeting when it is most dear —
> 'Tis gone while we but say ' 'tis here'."

Trimness may be here, and some approach to primness; but here and elsewhere in his work we find not
the cold, thin blood of a Pope, but the warm, red
blood of a Cavalier. This heat and exuberance sometimes, in fact, led him to shout a licentious note; but
in later life we find him possessed of the good sense
to be ashamed of this and to repent it sincerely. All
in all he pleased his day exceedingly well — four editions of his poems were issued between 1640 and 1671
— and all in all the day pleased him just as well. He
was, indeed, an " idle singer of an empty day," pos-
sessing some of the folly and false glitter of the age,
a trifle too indolent to imitate the pedantry of
Waller, a trifle too worldly to know the spirituality
of Donne, but too much of an artist to be satisfied

[15] *Select Beauties of Ancient English Poetry,* **Vol. I.**

with rough-and-ready, "hit-or-miss" effects. A
violent lover, but a careful singer, he won the usual
reward of the day — the hearts of numerous ladies
— and while Lovelace and many another Cavalier
crept away to languish in despair, he himself might
truly boast, at least temporarily:

> "But I did enter, and enjoy
>   What happy lovers prove,
> For I could kiss, and sport, and toy,
>   And taste those sweets of love."

"Tom" Carew, as even King Charles called him,
knew not so well where to stop as did Waller and
Herrick; he possessed less judgment, perhaps, in several poetic matters than they, but have they surpassed him in fervor and tenderness? His wit was
pointed, and yet he was ever careful in his use of it.
For he loved men and women, such as he knew, and
cared not to wound. In his gallantry, his sentiment,
his ideals, his use of verbal melody, his forms of
verse, his portrayal, literary and personal, of his
day, he represents a connecting link between Ben
Jonson and Prior, and hence to Pope. But of all
this he knew little and cared less. Bowing gallantly
to right and left, and with most tender glances toward the ladies, he leads us gently, unwittingly, perhaps, through that period when the luxuriance and
the hearty freedom of the Elizabethans were slowly
changing into the brilliance and cold restraint of the
classical days.

EDMUND WALLER

(1605 — 1687)

In an ancient parish graveyard at Beaconsfield, in
Buckinghamshire, there is a time-worn stone bearing
the name " Edmund Waller " and the words " *Inter
poetas sui temporis facile princeps.*" Such is fame.
Epitaphs do not, of course, come under the literature of fact — they generally belong to the more
entertaining field of fiction — but here in the vener-
able country churchyard that Latin inscription was
carved in all true faith and sincerity. The man
sleeping beneath the stone had for more than eighty
years lived through one of the stormiest eras in English history, had sung carefully his slender repertoire,
and had gone to the grave with the firm conviction
that the people's belief in his greatness was correct.
And Time has scarcely left him a name.

Fame's fickle ways are often difficult to explain;
but as we read the story of " time-serving " Edmund
Waller the reason for his present-day obscurity is
not hidden from us. He was born in his father's
mansion in Hertfordshire, in 1605, and started the
journey of life with wealth and influential connec-
tions. The father belonged to a family of wealthy
landowners, while the mother, though a Royalist,

was related rather closely to the important Cromwell family. The parents early removed to Beaconsfield, and there in that peaceful community Waller spent his happiest days, tuned and retuned his unimpassioned song, and at length returned to the dust. As a boy he attended Eton and King's College, Cambridge; but at the age of sixteen he had left such youthful business and was sitting as a member of Parliament. 'After all, however, the halls of law had but little charm for him in those days; for it seems that as soon as he had married the wealthy and pretty Anne Banks, and had paid his fine for doing so without her guardian's consent, he retired to the Beaconsfield home and prepared to spend long years in quiet domestic happiness. But the beautiful young wife died within three years (1634) and for a time the poet seemed utterly disconsolate.

Since the time, however, "when man's mind runneth not to the contrary" widowers, and widows too, have been able to recover from the shock of this bereavement, and thus it was with Waller. For four years he strove in vain to win the sweet-faced Lady Dorothea Sidney, the "Sacharissa" of his once admired love lyrics. The Lady Dorothea married another, and as there was little sincere passion in the poet's courtship he readily recovered from this shock, also. Years afterwards she asked him when he would again write such poetry to her. His answer betrayed his cold-blooded wit: "When you are as young, madam, and as handsome as you were then." And yet he had once declared,

"But for Sacharissa I
Do not only grieve, but die!"

"When he had lost all hopes of Sacharissa," says
Dr. Johnson, " he looked around for an easier conquest and gained a lady of the family of Bresse, or
Breaux. . . . He doubtless praised some whom
he would have been afraid to marry, and perhaps
married one whom he would have been ashamed to
praise." [1] And yet, if old Aubrey's description be
true, our poet was rather lucky to gain any sort of
helpmeet. "He is," says the plain-spoken biog-
rapher, "of somewhat above a middle stature, thin
body, not at all robust, fine, thin skin, his face
somewhat of an olivaster; his hayre frizzed of a
brownish colour; full eye, popping out and working;
ovall faced, his forehead high and full of wrinkles.
His head but small, braine very hott and apt to be
cholerique. . . . He is something magisteriall,
and haz a great mastership of the English language
. . . He haz but a tender, weake body, but was always very temperate . . . (quaere Samuel But-
ler) made him damnable drunke at Somerset-house,
where at the water-stayres he fell downe and had a
cruell fall. 'Twas pity to use such a sweet swan
so inhumanly . . . he will oftentimes be guilty
of mispelling in English. He writes a lamentably
bad hand, as bad as the scratching of a hen." [2]

During his years of poetical love-making with
Sacharissa he was taking no small interest in the na-

[1] *Lives of the English Poets.*
[2] Aubrey's *Brief Lives.*

tion's political activities. He was frequently in Parliament, was making numerous speeches, more effective in their display of wit than in their ability to win votes, and was writing complimentary verses of a calculating nature to my lords and ladies. Politically he was a weather-cock — like Lowell's Gineral C, he had been on every side that gave either place or pelf — and to-day we are disgusted when we see side by side his *Panegyric to My Lord Protector* and his *Death of the Late Usurper, O. C.* But a ready wit saved him from all embarrassments arising from such inconsistency. When Charles II came into his own, Waller welcomed him with the usual flattering lines, and when called to task by the king for having written better verses to Cromwell, instantly replied, " Sire, poets succeed better in fiction than in truth."

But even a weather-vane is battered in a tornado, and those were tornado days in English history. All the world knows the story of how the kings and the Parliament were browbeating each other in a desperate struggle to rule or ruin, and all the world knows, too, how the divine rights of kingship suffered a decisive shock. Waller, if he had any really sincere views on political matters, was against innovations, and thus it happened in that year of suspicion and anger, 1643, that he was siding with the king against the loud-talking rowdies in the Commons. Then came the exciting " Waller's Plot." It was all so romantic — and so disastrous. Waller was to see that the Royalists of London were gathered into an army; the Earl of Bath was to be re-

leased ·from the Tower and made general of the
forces; King Charles, with three thousand soldiers,
was to be within a few miles of the city; the great
metropolis was to be stormed from within and from
without — and wouldn't the Commons be surprised!

The most surprised man was Edmund Waller.
Arrested for treason, he immediately informed upon
all his associates and caused three of them to be ex-
ecuted. On July 4 he was brought before Parliament to make the remarkable speech that Clarendon
declares saved his life; on July 14 he was pronounced
incapable of ever again entering Parliament. He
was placed in the Tower, where he remained until
November of the next year, and in September, 1644,
he was in such despair that he offered to pay ten
thousand pounds for the opportunity to live. Then
came the judgment — a fine of ten thousand pounds
and banishment to France.

But how easily those gallants of the old days recovered from the trials and tribulations of this
world! Just before crossing the channel he found
a new love in the Mary Basey, or Brasse, mentioned
by Johnson, a lady of Oxfordshire, married her,
and lived serenely with her in France until fortune
turned a smiling face. In November, 1651, Parliament revoked his sentence, and once more he took
his part in the movement of the day, won favor from
both Protector and king, tuned his somewhat stilted
song for an admiring audience, and so lived in comparative peace until the tombstone maker carved
" *facile princeps* " in the churchyard. It is said

that he acted a more manly part after his return
from exile, and even dared to speak out boldly to the
narrow-minded Parliament for toleration toward the
persecuted Quakers.   Doubtless, weather-vane though
he had been, he had learned at last to be wise rather
than cunning, had learned the well-expressed truth
of his own poem, *Of the Last Verses in the Book:*

" The soul's dark cottage, battered and decayed,
  Lets in new light through chinks that time has made."

It has always appeared to me that this man should
be included among the songsters whom Johnson
dubbed the " Metaphysical Poets."   And in saying
this I do not forget the words of Edmund Gosse:
" The ingenuity of Waller is entirely distinct from
that metaphysical wit for which his contemporaries
were famous."   But should not Edmund Gosse have
begun that statement with the words, " in his *later*
days?"   For Waller was a literary weather-vane
as well as a political one, and the lyric poetry of his
youth was not the precise verse of his old age.   Hear
these words:

" Go lovely rose,
  Tell her that wastes her time and me,
    That now she knows
  ,When I resemble her to thee,
  How sweet and fair she seems to be."

Do those far-famed lines sound of the spirit of Suckling and Carew or of Dryden and Pope?   And,
again, note the song to Flavia:

" 'Tis not your beauty can engage
       My wary heart:
The sun, in all his pride and rage,
       Has not the art;
And yet he shines as bright as you,
If brightness could our souls subdue."

No, Edmund Waller, in his early life, wrote as his
friends wrote, and his friends were the "metaphysical" singers. But afar off he saw the signs of
change, and, prudent and self-guarding as he was,
he early prepared for the new song. For Waller
clung to no ideals, no dear things of olden days; he
longed for immediate applause; and he framed his
style as his audience demanded. Unblushingly he
pilfered what he considered best from the older poets,
remodeled it, "formalized" it, brought it strictly
up to date, and presented to the court reader the
old wine in new bottles. And the bottles cannot be
denied a certain pleasing primness. In the songs
of his youth he allowed himself much of the license
found in the other Cavalier singers, but as the fad
of classicism grew, he grew with it, and in time English readers forgot the freer lyrics of his youthful
hours and remembered only the smoothly turned
couplets of mature days. When the Restoration
came, he and Cowley had been before the public
more than thirty years; the wild young rakes of their
earlier days had returned to dust, and the songs of
these dusty rakes had passed into a certain obscurity. This was Waller's opportunity. He re-sang
their songs. He washed the rouge from Carew's and

Herrick's and Suckling's sweetheart, snipped off a few yards of her suggestive lace, taught her to put primness into her thoughts, and presented her with great applause to the admiring court. True, she could no longer sing, but she could moralize; hence the applause. The lyrical days had gone, and now cynical, brilliant verses paced mechanically, two by two, through the glittering halls.

And yet something of the old tone remained. How extravagant even Waller's gallantry seems! Looking upon his lady's girdle, he exclaimed:

> " It was my heaven's extremest sphere!
> .   .   .   .
> " Give me but what this ribband bound,
>   Take all the rest the sun goes round."

Does it sound so very unlike the poets of his youth? And is there not an echo of Sir John Suckling in the temporariness of such love as that offered to Phyllis?

> " Let not you and I enquire
>   What has been our past desire;
>   On what shepherds you have smiled,
>   Or what nymphs I have beguiled;
>   Leave it to the planets, too,
>   What we shall hereafter do:
>   For the joys we now may prove,
>   Take advice of present love."

After all, however, Waller scarcely belonged to any school. Pliant as he was, he served as a connecting link between the poets of the Jonson era and the poets of the Restoration. He partook of the qualities of both; and in his minute weighing of words, skillful arrangement of phrases and ever-conscious design, he produced a polished compactness which greatly influenced, even if it did not found, the school of Dryden and Pope. Well might Dryden say: " Edmund Waller first showed us to conclude the sense most commonly in distichs; which in the verse of those before him runs on for so many lines together that the reader is out of breath to overtake it."

Like his day, he was highly artificial. Even his lengthy religious poems, such as the poetical reflections on the Lord's Prayer, lack the warmth and fervor expected to-day of such works. Even his love verses are frigid; but, as Gosse points out, " if they do not take the heart by storm, they beleaguer it with great strategic art and an infinite show of patience." [3] Ambitious Waller loved not with his heart but with his intellect, if he loved at all, and therefore, in the words of worldly-wise Walpole, " he excelled in painting ladies in enamel, but could not succeed in portraits in oil, large as life." [4] Only love produces masterpieces.

Conscious art, then, was the characteristic of the man. The slender book of his verse shows many and many a sign of the felt brush and chamois-skin; but, ah, how little of heart, of sincere passion, of stern belief is there! The full-flushed sunset of Shakes-

[3] Ward's *English Poets*, Vol. II, p. 272.
[4] *Letters*, ed. Cunningham, Vol. III, p. 564.

peare and Jonson had passed; the chill, steely dawn
of a Pope was almost at hand. Waller had memories
of that gorgeous sunset; but such a day had gone
forever, and with little of regret he hastened to meet
the first pale rays of another dawn. Thus Edmund
Waller turned and veered with each gust of popular
taste, saying as he veered:

> " How small a part of time they share,
> That are so wondrous sweet and fair."

SIR JOHN SUCKLING

(1609 — 1642)

Frank, impudent Sir John Suckling! He was the slave of no woman, no, not one. Why, exclaimed he,

> " If of herself she will not love,
>   Nothing can make her;
>   The devil take her!"

How he reasoned it all out — this madness called love! He had studied the psychology of it every whit, not from books, not from philosophical lectures, but from real experiments, from experience itself. The symptoms were so plain to him:

> " If when she appears i' th' room
>   Thou dost not quake, and art struck dumb,
>   And in striving this to cover,
>   Dost not speak thy words twice over,
>   Know this,
>   Thou lov'st amiss,
>   And to love true,
> Thou must begin again, and love anew."

He was, indeed, a valiant lover — for a day or two. In his time, boasted he, he had won his many a prize — of fair dames' hearts — by many an ingenious

and daring adventure; he had undermined her heart
" by whispering in the ear," or

> " brought down
> Great cannon-oaths, and shot
> A thousand thousand to the town."

Who was this unabashed gallant that bade the
ladies love him, but told them frankly that he was
like to forget them day after to-morrow? Quaint
old John Aubrey, who was of his own century, says:
" He was the greatest gallant of his time, and the
greatest gamester, both for bowling and cards, so
that no shopkeeper would trust him for 6 *d*, as to-
day, for instance, he might, by winning, be worth 200
li., the next day he might not be worth half so much,
or perhaps be sometimes *minus nihilo.* Sir William
[Davenant] (who was his intimate friend, and loved
him intirely) would say that Sir John, when he was
at his lowest ebbe in gameing, I mean when unfortunate, then would make himselfe most glorious in
apparell, and sayd that it exalted his spirits, and
that he had best luck when he was most gallant,
and his spirits were highest." [1] Then, speaking of
the happy-go-lucky poet's appearance, Aubrey continues: " He was of middle stature and slight
strength, brisque round eie, reddish fac't and red
nose (ill liver), his head not very big, his hayre a
kind of sand colour; his beard turned-up naturally,
so that he had brikse and gracefull looke." [2] We

1 Aubrey's *Brief Lives.*
2 Aubrey's *Brief Lives.*

may still see his portrait by Van Dyck — a handsome, alert fellow in gorgeous garments, with long, fair curls hanging down to his shoulders, with red lips of manly firmness, and with a pair of blue eyes that had looked keenly, and victoriously, into many a damsel's blushing face. The picture shows something of the dare-devilry that marked his day; but, ah, how little it foretells those last dark hours of confusion and despair!

He was born at Whitton, in Middlesex, late in 1608, or in January, 1609, entered Trinity College, Cambridge, in 1623, and was early brought up to court by his versatile and well-beloved father, Sir John Suckling, Secretary of State. The usual tales of youthful precocity are not lacking. " He had so pregnant a Genius," says Gerard Langbaine, " that he spoke Latin at Five Years Old, and writ it at Nine Years of Age. His Skill in Languages and Musick was Remarkable; but above all his Poetry took with the People, whose Souls were polished by the Charms of the Muses." [3]   Be that as it may, it is certain that the silks and satins, rouge and powder of Cavaliers and lofty dames abashed him not one whit. If we may take as true the words of his admiring friend, Sir William Davenant, he " for his accomplishments and ready witt was the bull that was most bayted; his repartee being most sparkling when set on and provoked."

But the perfumed air of the palace seems to have

3 Langbaine, *An Account of the English Dramatick Poets,* p. 496.

been rather stifling to the hot-blooded young gallant, and we find him between his nineteenth and twenty-third year wandering over Europe, marching with the army of Gustavus Adolphus, fighting with astounding recklessness in Silesia, and at length quitting the army because *war did not offer enough variety!* What a full life physically those courtiers of the old day led! We of the Puritan inheritance can scarcely realize it and certainly cannot appreciate it. Men drank deeply, swore valiantly, loved madly, and drained the stirrup-cup with a smack. For six years wild Sir John, now in London, lived a life so profligate that he almost squandered one of the greatest fortunes of his century. Then he went to Bath on the pretext of living frugally — God save the mark! — and made himself so conspicuous by his mock repentance that the king begged him to return to the erstwhile lonesome court. "Bonnie King Charlie" had every reason to love the spendthrift knight, for many a thousand pounds of Sir John's had accompanied the witty mots and wild pranks of his youthful spirits. In the troubled days of 1639 Sir John, with all the esthetic enthusiasm of a poet and the dashing gallantry of a soldier, had gathered his troop of a hundred handsome Cavaliers, had arrayed them bravely in scarlet and white, aye, had spent twelve thousand pounds on their accoutrement, and then had seen them, at the first sight of the bare-legged Scotch army, flee to a man! It was a great shock to Sir John's sense of honor and pride; but the king knew his intentions were good, forgave him, and loved him just the same. It is said that at this point in his career he thought of marrying a woman of great wealth; but, alas, " a rival, strong of arm, cudgelled him till he agreed to renounce all claims upon the golden prize," [4] and he spent his days a bachelor.

Somebody—maybe he himself—had deluded Suckling into the idea that he could write a play, and he made four valiant and vicious attempts at the business. They are miserable stuff — even his best friends laughed at them — but in the midst of all the dragging lines and watery sentimentality occur some lyrics that make us thankful he lived and sang. English literature would not willingly spare such songs as " Why so pale and wan, fond lover? " and " Hast thou seen the down in the air? " Yet, the hot young knight scorned the title of poet. He wrote plays simply because it was the style for all fashionable gentlemen to attempt it, not for money, not for fame, but only to see if he could. Life, life abounding, was far more to him than literature.

But now the dark turning in that flood of life was at hand. His fortune was well nigh spent; his " lines had fallen in hard places." Suddenly he was accused — justly or unjustly, we know not — of attempting to rescue Stafford from the Tower. He fled to France and then to Spain. The world will

---

[4] Gardner's *History of England from the Accession of James I to the Outbreak of the Civil War*, Vol. IV, p. 311.

never know accurately what happened behind those
closed doors of the Spanish Inquisition. We know
only that poor John Suckling, poet, soldier and
great-hearted gentleman, fell into its clutches, and
came forth haggard, vacant-eyed, an imbecile.
" Reduced, at length, in fortune and dreading to
encounter poverty, which his habits and temper were
little calculated to endure, hurled from his rank in
society, an alien and perhaps friendless, his energies
at length gave way to the complicated wretchedness
of his situation, and he contemplated an act which
he had himself condemned in others." [5] Creeping
back to Paris, he struggled to recall the thoughts
that had once been his; but it was all a vain dream
about dreams, and a phial of poison gave him lasting sleep. So passed, in his thirty-fourth year, one
who was born to rule, but did not — one handsome,
bold, versatile, generous, ever popular, king of good
fellows.

> " The blithest throat that ever carolled love
>   In music made of morning's merriest heart,
> Glad Suckling stumbled from his seat above,
>   And reeled on slippery roads of alien art." [6]

Suckling's poetry should not be considered apart
from his life. And we have seen that he considered
the latter far more important than the former. So
little, indeed, did he care for his literary productions
that possibly but three of them — *Sessions of the*

[5] Alfred Suckling, ed. *Suckling's Works.*
[6] Swinburne's *James Shirley.*

Poets (1637), *Aglaura* (1638), and the *Ballad on a Wedding* (1640) — were published during his own lifetime. But there were friends — enthusiastic, long-remembering friends — who, mindful of his winning ways, his brilliant wit, and his altogether lovable personality, resolved that his name should not perish from among men. Within four years after his death, therefore, they gathered the scattered fragments of his songs and sayings into a volume which they magnanimously called *Fragmenta Aurea: a Collection of all the Incomparable Pieces Written by Sir John Suckling*. We, who have never seen those blue eyes of his or heard the hearty voice that cheered King Charles, cannot exactly see the propriety of that word "incomparable"; and yet in the thirty years extending from 1646 to 1676 seven editions of *Fragmenta Aurea* were exhausted. Tastes in poetry, as in love, change, and, in the words of Sir John himself,

> "Men rise away, and scarce say grace,
> Or civilly once thank the face
> That did invite; but seek another place."

Change in taste, however, rarely affects a good lyric. The simple sentiment that appeals to the heart, the rhythmic rise and fall that appeals to the ear, the genial harmony of phrase and feeling — these when skillfully used must grant immortality to any song, no matter how slight its contents. De Quincey once said: " The artifice and machinery of rhetoric furnishes in its degree as legitimate a basis for intellectual pleasure as any other: that

the pleasure is of an inferior order can no more at-
taint the idea or model of the composition than it
can impeach the excellence of an epigram that it is
not a tragedy." [7]   Just so it is with Suckling.
There is very little of the dramatic in him, very little of the thinker, very little of imagination, and
even less of heartfelt sentiment; but, ah, that careless grace of expression, that gaiety, that non-
chalance! He has no time for tears of repentance;
there are too many ladies in the world for him to
waste his days at that. "The path," says Freder-
ick Stokes, "which Suckling's verse takes never
scales sublime heights, but runs through fields where
music and laughter are heard, where beauty is seen,
and where there are occasional stormy days." [8]   He
can be as delicate as the sweetest of the ladies; but,
man of action that he is, he prefers to be speaking
out loud and cheerily, to "be carving of the best," to

"Rudely call for the last course 'fore the rest."

It is this brusqueness, this contempt for mournful sentimentality, that makes Sir John Suckling so
refreshing among the lovers of his day. "He
comes upon a herd of scented fops with careless natural grace, and an odor of morning flowers upon
him. You know not which would have been most
delighted with his compliments, the dairy maid or
the duchess." [9]   Hazlitt remarks that his "letters
are full of habitual good sense," and so is his poetry

[7] *Historical Essays*, II.
[8] Ed. *Poems of Suckling*, p. 13.
[9] Leigh Hunt, *Wit and Humor*, p. 216.

— generally. He speaks as a man of experience, not as

> " Some youth that has not made his story."

What woman, he impudently asks, as he looks straight into the eyes of the bepowdered court ladies — what woman is worth mourning over? His fellow-singer, Lovelace, looks upon the same bright faces, or, more correctly, just *one* of them, and becomes tragically constant; but Suckling smiles knowingly, and frankly avows his inconstancy:

> " I'll court you all to serve my turn."

'And what effect had this upon the feminine heart? Let a modern literary woman speak: " Sir John Suckling is not to be trusted for good behavior through many stanzas, but how enchantingly gay he is! The utter frankness of his hilarity does something toward atoning for his coarseness. We are quite sure that he is never worse than his words, and even suspect that he is not altogether so desperate a rake as he sometimes pretends." [10] Such views as his were sure to win the day among seventeenth century courtiers, and at length we find Suckling's verses so greatly changing the style of poetical love-making from the long-faced, " dying " sentimentality of his own times that amorous poetry becomes in the days of the Restoration almost bestial in its frankness.

[10] Harriet Preston, "The Latest Songs of Chivalry." *Atlantic Monthly,* Vol. XLIII, p. 20.

Little time had he for polishing verses. War and woman were abroad in the land, and he was extremely busy. Some of his poems are so careless as to be not only unpoetic but almost unintelligible. And yet how ingenious he could be! Nowhere in English poetry is there a better sustained piece of light foolery than his *Ballad upon a Wedding*, with its enchanting bride:

> " Her mouth so small when she does speak,
> Thou'dst swear her teeth her words did break."

That same ingenuity, too, is shown not only in the general air of gaiety, but in the difficult recurrence of rhymes and the novel scheme of verse and stanza forms.

But enough of forms and verse schemes. The play's the thing — the play of ideas, the play of sparkling words, the play of Sir John Suckling's impudent wit. See him strut, smilingly, confidently, among the unflattered but secretly admiring damsels, while he hums:

> " I am confirmed a woman can
> Love this or that or any man."

RICHARD CRASHAW

(1613 (?) — 1649)

To some men God gives a peace of heart sur-
passing all knowledge. Such a man was Richard
Crashaw, saintly priest and enraptured singer of
things divine. His friend and editor, Thomas Car,[1]
described him as one

" Who was belov'd by all, disprais'd by none:
To witt, being pleas'd with all things, he pleas'd all,
Nor would he give, nor take offence."

And even those who rather wished to hate him for
embracing Catholicism could not but speak well of
him. Even Cowley, who had become almost puritanical in his own life, but who, nevertheless, despised
the Puritans with a scorn exceeded only by his hatred of Romanism, loved this godly worshipper with
all his heart, and wrote with a warmth hardly to be
expected of him:

" His faith perhaps in some nice traits might
Be wrong; his life, I'm sure, was in the right.
And I myself a Catholic will be,
So far at least, great Saint, to pray to thee.
Hail, bard triumphant! and some care bestow
On us, the poets militant below!" [2]

[1] Editor of *Carmen Deo Nostro.*
[2] *On the Death of Mr. Crashaw.*

Crashaw's was a life without storms, seemingly without spiritual conflict. All his days were filled with a childlike faith in a beneficent Creator, and while others struggled onward through anguish and tears to their eternal crown, his soul soared with never a doubt, never a self-depreciation, never a lapse from joyous and even rapturous belief. He was never an ascetic; he was simply a glad-hearted devotee. He could not understand puritanical austerity; for his was an untrammeled joy in every beautiful thing that God had created — an abiding faith that the same Hand that shaped these creatures of loveliness intended man to be just as lovely and just as happy. To him was granted

" A happy soul that all the way
To heaven hath a summer day."

Before, however, we enter too intimately into the nature of this glad singer and his songs, let us note the few incidents in the brief years of his life here. His father, William Crashaw, was a poet and a clergyman of Whitechapel, and there in that ancient section of the London labyrinth the boy was born in 1613. He attended Charterhouse School, and passed in 1631 to Pembroke College, Cambridge, where he early began to be recognized as a scholar among scholars. He translated with readiness Greek, Hebrew, Latin, Spanish, and Italian; he was especially versed in Greek and Latin poetry; he was skillful in music, dancing, painting, and engraving.

In 1637 he was awarded a fellowship in Peterhouse in recognition of his merit.

But there he now came under a great influence which transformed his opinions of life and caused all his brilliant accomplishments to seem vain, even if harmless, frivolities. That influence was Nicholas Ferrar, the devout thinker who so strongly attracted the university men of the early seventeenth century. Learned man of science though he was, popularly known far and near, able to secure for himself offices of power and authority, this deep meditator, Nicholas Ferrar, at length renounced all earthly ambitions, gathered a little group of religious enthusiasts, and retiring into Huntingdonshire founded at Little Giddings a community which lived not for this world but for the world not made with hands, eternal in the heavens. The spirit of this leader profoundly affected Richard Crashaw, and we find that after 1638 the young poet devoted little of his time and energy to aught else save religious meditations and religious activities. Then began that life so full of the spirit of the early saints — a life some hint of the gentle sweetness of which is given in his preface to his *Steps to the Temple:* " Reader, we style his sacred poems *Steps to the Temple,* and aptly, for in the temple of God, under his wing, he led his life in Saint Mary's Church, near Saint Peter's College; there he lodged under Tertullian's roof of angels; there he made his nest more gladly than David's swallows near the house of God, where, like a primitive saint, he offered more prayers in the night than others usually offer in the day; there he penned these poems, steps for happy souls to climb to heaven by."

Now, in seventeenth-century days there was one sure haven of peace for such a soul. Crashaw loved the moral with the fervor of an idealist; he loved the beautiful with the eye of an artist; his soul longed for a union of the two. And at length he felt that he had found such a union within the Catholic fold. Slowly, indeed, the conviction grew upon him; but as he read the heroic lives of the early saints and studied the order, the customs, and the symbolism of the mighty Roman Church, the vastness and the majesty of the institution seized upon his imagination, and he at last found himself gladly, whole-heartedly, a believer in the persecuted faith. Nor did he fail to suffer his share of that persecution. When, in 1643, Parliament demanded that all monuments of superstition be removed from the churches and that fellows of the universities be required to take the Oath of the Solemn League and Covenant, Richard Crashaw refused to speak the binding words. That which he knew to be inevitable followed — the loss of his fellowship. Never once, however, did he lose his abiding faith in the ideal, the far-seen vision of perfection which has sustained so many leaders, whether religious or secular. He gloried, as his own words declare, in

" Life that dares send
    A challenge to his end,
    And when it comes, says, ' Welcome, Friend! ' " [3]
  [3] *Wishes to His Mistress.*

Left without employment, he departed from England forever in 1646 and went to France to seek some means of support. There, in great distress, he walked the streets of Paris for days, finding no friend, no sympathizer. He now had become a member of the Catholic Church, and his former associates either suspected him of having pecuniary advantages in view, or, with puritanical Prynne, considered him a "fickle shuttlecock." Could those who were accusing him of treason for money have seen him in the streets of Paris, surely their accusations would have ceased. Here at length Cowley, the strict conformist, found him, looked upon him with love, even though a Catholic, and introduced him to the exiled Queen Henrietta Maria; and once more Fortune smiled upon the gentle, strong-hearted idealist. In 1648 the Queen recommended him to the higher authorities of the Church; he was given service with a cardinal at Rome, and at length, in April, 1649, he was appointed sub-canon at the cathedral in Loretto. Now, at last, he had reached his heart's desire; he could spend his days in rapt meditation and in joyous songs to his Maker. Four months later he was lying dead in the ancient Italian city. And Cowley, with the sorrow of a brother, wrote of him:

" Poet and Saint! to thee alone are given
   The two most sacred names of earth and heaven,
   The hard and rarest union which can be
   Next that of God-head with humanitie." [4]

[4] *On the Death of Mr. Crashaw.*

The poetic genius in Crashaw flowered early. While still a college student, in 1634, he published his volume of Latin poems, *Epigrammatum Sacrorum Liber*, and one famous verse in it —

" The conscious water saw its God and blushed "—

is worthy of a far older and more famous singer.   In 1646, just as he was leaving England, his *Steps to the Temple: Sacred Poems, with other Delights of the Muses*, appeared, and an audience, especially among Catholic readers, was assured him.   In fact, the collection became so well known that a French edition entitled *Carmen Deo Nostro*, with twelve fine engravings designed by Crashaw himself, was published in 1682 and was widely sold and widely praised.   And yet the poems had been written, for the most part, before the loss of the fellowship in 1643, and their author was so modest in his estimation of these youthful verses that he called them but the " steps " to Herbert's famous *Temple*, which had appeared in 1633.

The last pages of the book, comprising the " other delights of the Muses," consist of secular poems, dealing even with such earthly subjects as love for woman.   But it is in the preceding pages, the *Steps to the Temple*, that we see the real Crashaw.   As stated before, he had read the beautiful, even if fanciful, " lives " of the early saints, and many of the rhapsodies by the devout churchmen of the warm-blooded Southern lands, and the spirit of these works had become his.   Especially had he learned to love and to imitate the ecstatic compositions of St. Teresa, to whom, by the way, are written two of his most stirring hymns. How literary traditions link into one another! Says Coleridge of these two songs: " These verses were ever present to my mind whilst writing the second part of *Christabel;* if, indeed, by some subtle process of mind they did not suggest the first thought of the whole poem." [5] From St. Teresa to Coleridge! But well might the poems of Crashaw suggest the mystical; for " sensuous mysticism " [6] was the very soul of the man. His was a fervor, a sentiment, a wonder, akin to that more modern mystic, Shelley.

Now, this characteristic of Crashaw easily led to some obvious defects. Masson has pointed out that throughout this poet's work there is often " a certain flowing effeminacy of expression, a certain languid sensualism of fancy, or, to be still more particular, an almost cloying use of the words ' sweet,' ' dear,' and their cognates, in reference to all kinds of objects." [7] The tendency may, of course, be excused to some extent by noting that such was the prevalent spirit at the time among devotional writers of France and Italy, and also a not uncommon expression of affection for their religion by devout Catholics not only of Southern Europe but of England itself. And we are more than likely to forget this pardonable weakness when we realize the height of feeling, the ecstasy, attained by Crashaw

[5] *Letters and Conversation.*
[6] Palgrave *Treasury of Sacred Songs,* Note. p. 342.
[7] *Life of Milton,* Vol. I, ch. vi.

— an ecstasy difficult indeed to understand and seemingly extravagant in this day, when an extremely personal God and an extremely personal religion appear to be declining. Can we feel the rush of emotion which must have come to him in this *Song* to Christ from *Carmen Deo Nostro?*

> " O Love, I am thy sacrifice,
>   Be still triumphant, blessed eyes;
>   Still shine on me, fair suns, that I
>   Still may behold though still I die."

But, despite the thrilling fervor of the man, there are in his work disappointing qualities which, from an artistic point of view, cannot be overlooked. He does not seem to strain for effect, and yet his conceits are often most tasteless. The " sister baths " and " portable oceans " of his *Magdalene* have long been considered unpardonable, and other examples equally bad might easily be found. He seems to have written with a whirl and rush and scarcely ever to have revised, and the wild struggle of his intellect to conquer and interpret his passion leaves too often, indeed, only such confused effects as those in the almost hopeless stanza from his *Hymn of the Nativity:*

> " She sings thy tears asleep, and dips
>   Her kisses in thy weeping eye;
>   She spreads the red leaves of thy lips,
>   That in their buds yet blushing lie.
>   She 'gainst those mother diamonds tries
>   The points of her young eagle's eyes."

Here, in his intense visualization of the subject, he
no longer sees in proper proportions; but, instead,
the images, like his passions, confuse and bewilder
him, leaving him no tongue for his onrushing
thoughts. Where there are such heights of emotion
there are bound to be lapses into slovenliness and
commonplaceness. And just here is one of the surprising qualities of Crashaw. For many lines he
wanders along in a veritable slough of despond, as
far as beauty of thought is concerned, when suddenly the wonders of his theme kindle his imagination, and then come lines of soaring rapture scarcely
excelled in all lyric poetry. So it is in *The Flaming
Heart*, where, after a succession of lines commonplace enough, he bursts forth with a torrent of ring-
ing words that in their passionate spiritedness are
scarcely equalled in the literature of England.

Well may Swinburne speak of his " dazzling in-
tricacy and affluence in refinement." Too often,
perhaps, he imitates the unreal quaintness and conceits of his Italian favorites, especially Marino; but
in spite of exaggerations, far-fetched metaphors,
and wild ecstasies, he is seldom tiresome. He may,
indeed, use too many repetitions, as in his *Mistress*,
where he evolves numerous expressions for the one
wish that his imaginary sweetheart may not paint.
He may even deal in punning conceits, as in the
same poem, where he speaks of

> " A cheek where grows
> More than a morning rose:
> Which to no *box* his being owes."

Granted that these fanciful twists of thought do not represent the highest poetic art, it must be admitted, nevertheless, that many of them are exceedingly well turned.

> " I wish her store
>   Of worth may leave her poor
>   Of wishes; and I wish — no more."

And let those who think that he cannot rid himself of his conceits and sound the iron tone of Milton's verse, read these lines from his description of hell and its king:

" Below the bottom of the great abyss,
    There, where one center reconciles all things,
    The world's profound heart pants; there placed is
    Mischief's old master; close about him clings
    A curl'd knot of embracing snakes, that kiss
    His correspondent cheeks: these loathsome strings
        Hold the perverse prince in eternal ties
        Fast bound, since first he forfeited the skies.

.   .   .   .

" His eyes, the sullen dens of Death and Night,
    Startle the dull air with a dismal red:
    Such his fell glances, as the fatal light
    Of staring comets, that look kingdoms dead.
    From his black nostrils and blue lips, in spite
    Of Hell's own stink, a worser stench is spread.
        His breath Hell's lightning is: and each deep
            groan
        Disdains to think that Heav'n thunders alone."

And yet this is the singer of whom Pope once wrote:

" I take this poet to have writ like a gentleman, that is, at leisure hours and more to keep out of idleness than to establish a reputation, so that nothing regular or just can be expected from him." [8]

Pope has not been the only severe critic of this glory-singing poet; there have been a number, and some have been authoritative men of letters. Hazlitt, for instance, declared in 1820 that " Crashaw was a hectic enthusiast in religion and in poetry, and erroneous in both." [9]   But Sara Coleridge, writing twenty-seven years later, considered his poetry " more truly poetical than any other except Milton and Dante." [10]   He has never been a popular poet, nor is he likely ever to be. His religion was against him in the England of his own day. The tendency of his age toward the " classical " restraint and coldness of Pope was never his tendency; and rapturous meditations on divine subjects found no place in the mighty industrial era which the nineteenth century opened. Consequently, Crashaw has been neglected. All this, however, does not condemn him as a poet of small genius; he simply was unfortunate in his day. It required a brave soul to sing as he did in such a period, and, as Gosse has noted, his works present the only important contribution to English literature made by a pronounced Catholic, embodying Catholic doctrine, during the whole of the seventeenth century." [11]   And

[8] Letter to H. Cromwell, Dec. 17, 1710.
[9] Lectures on the Literature of the Age of Elizabeth.
[10] Memoirs and Letters, p. 320.
[11] Seventeenth Century Studies, p. 143.

he sang with a noble sweetness that is worthy of his bravery. Injured somewhat by the false tastes of his age, he nevertheless, by sheer enthusiasm, by sheer impetuosity of emotions, gained a largeness and loftiness of imagination, even a sublimity of view, that carried him far above the petty themes and petty thoughts of the hour, into the kingdom of sweetness and light. Well has Palgrave expressed the truth when he says: "Crashaw has a charm so unique, an imagination so nimble and subtle, phrases of such sweet and passionate felicity, that readers who . . . turn to his little book will find themselves surprised and delighted, in proportion to their sympathetic sense of poetry, when touched to its rarer and finer issues." [12]

Crashaw was so strangely different in heart and spirit from most of the other Royalist singers of his times. Like Keats and Shelley, he was not of this world. His noted contemporary, Herbert, was undoubtedly just as religious; but Herbert knew the world so well that he was sick of it, while Crashaw knew it not at all. Herbert feared the contamination of things earthly; Crashaw, in his innocence, loved to use earthly images in his worship of God. It was his delight " to revel in light, color, motion, and space," [13] and his very fault of enveloping his subject in the cloud of hints and inferences that rushed upon him was due to this joy in the creations of his Maker. How tender is his regard for the symbols of things spiritual!

[12] *Treasury of Sacred Songs*, p. 342.
[13] Schelling, *Seventeenth Century Lyrics*, p. 32.

Yet, this ardent affection for spiritual matters did not cause him to become wholly a hazy, rambling dreamer. He often looked at things with " a full, open, penetrative eye "; he saw his theme in a multitude of lights; his imagination seemed to find a universe in the humblest bit of the Creator's handicraft. Well has it been said that " he is fraught with suggestion — infinite suggestion." [14] But it is the suggestiveness of a child's fancy — a child whose wonder at and joy in the heavens has not been deadened by the rough handling of an intensely practical world. Hear the high-keyed note of rapture in the opening lines of *The Weeper:*

" Hail, sister springs!
Parents of silver-footed rills!
Ever-bubbling things!
Thawing crystal! Snowy hills,
Still spending, never spent! I mean
Thy fair eyes, sweet Magdalene!"

Crashaw is not a poet of fireside thoughts and domestic emotions in the sense that Wordsworth and Burns are. His are not the common sentiments of every-day life. No, his are the lofty, far-off chants of the echoing cathedral, over-gorgeous perhaps, fantastic perhaps, yet appealing with a strange, rich pathos to the soul of man. When he rises to rhapsody, as in the last lines of *On The Assumption of the Virgin Mary*, he thrills with a mingling of the fervor of the ancient psalms and the personal warmth of modern evangelical religion.

[14] Thompson, *The Academy*, Vol. LII, p. 427.

There is always some surprise in store for readers of this rapt singer. Sometimes it is the novelty of the poetic structure, sometimes the height of emotion, sometimes, as in *The Musician and the Nightingale*, the masterly power over words, and sometimes also, it must be confessed, the foolish fabric of his conceits. But when he feels the fire in his soul, how he rises above this weakness of the age! Then it is that he grasps the lyre with a master's hand, and, glowing with an oriental warmth, sings like the lover in the *Song of Solomon:*

"Whilst through the crystal orbs, clearer than they,
She climbs, and makes a far more milky way.
She's called again; hark how the dear immortal dove
Sighs to his silver mate, 'Rise up, my love,
　　Rise up, my fair, my spotless one,
　　The winter's past, the rain is gone;
　　The spring is come, the flowers appear,
　　No sweets, save thou, are wanting here.' "

This, then, is the half-forgotten bard, Richard Crashaw. Why he has become so neglected is difficult to understand. Not all the worthy singers have received a laurel. The age, the inclinations of the masses, the accidents of war and dynasty, the changes of industry, the social upheavals of humanity, the conquests of religions, the rise of a new and overshadowing genius — all these may leave a gifted poet obscure, forgotten, lonely in his dark nook. But he continues to be a gifted poet notwithstanding. Such an unfortunate is Crashaw. He must wait. Some day, perhaps, when the all-absorbing economic activities which began with the nineteenth century have spent their force, and men, tired of an over-wise world, shall creep back to the quiet holiness of the Mysterious One on High, the weary ones may turn once more to the vision-seeing Crashaw, and love with him the things not made with hands, eternal in the heavens.

RICHARD LOVELACE

(1618 — 1658)

He died in a cellar in Gunpowder Alley, near Shoe
Lane, London. And yet Anthony à Wood says he
was, as a young courtier, " accounted the most
amiable and beautiful person that ever eye beheld," [1]— so beautiful, in fact, that the admiring
ladies and envious nobles of the Caroline circle commonly called him Adonis. Brave-hearted Lovelace!
— he was as true and gentle as he was modest.
Hear Anthony à Wood speak again: " A person
also of innate modesty, virtue, and courtly deport-
ment, which made him then . . . when he retired
to the great city, much admired and adored by the
female sex . . . a person well vers'd in the
Greek and Latin poets, in music, whether practical
or theoretical, instrumental or vocal, and in other
things befitting a gentleman." [2] How different
was his quiet, unchanging nature from the careless,
impudent, shifting spirit of his braggadocio friend,
Sir John Suckling! What Saintsbury has said of
their lyrics might well be said of their lives: " The
songs remain yet unsurpassed as the most perfect
celebrations, in one case of chivalrous devotion, in

[1] Anthony à Wood, *Athenae Oxonienses*, Vol. II, p. 228.
[2] Wood, *Athenae Oxonienses*, Vol. II, p. 228.

the other of the coxcomb side of gallantry, that literature contains or is likely to contain." [3] Life was a tragedy to both brave knights; but while Suckling passed out with high dramatic effects that well became such a showy actor, poor Dick Lovelace ended in undeserved and undramatic misery and shame.

The son of Sir William Lovelace, he was born in a mansion at Woolwich, in Kent, was educated in Charterhouse School and at Gloucester Hall, Oxford. He early became the pet of royalty, and developed into an exquisitely beautiful, graceful grown-up child, a player, singer, dancer, and flatterer of coral lips and azure eyes. In him the gentle blood of royalty reached an ideal; in him, as Miss Mifford says, was " an impersonation of the Cavalier of the civil wars, with much to charm the reader and still more to captivate the fair." [4] But behind that soft manner and charming face was a spirit as true as steel. How full of daring deeds was that short life! When not actually in military service he was either plotting or in prison. We know that when the citizens of Kent signed their brave petition in behalf of Charles, and looked about for a man — not a mere knight, or soldier, or statesman, but a *man* — to carry that declaration to the Commons, Sir Richard Lovelace accepted the charge, presented the parchment to the maddened assembly, and marched calmly into that Westminster prison which he knew to be inevitable. Forty thousand

[3] *Elizabethan Literature,* p. 376.
[4] *Recollections of a Literary Life.*

pounds was the bail required for that bit of heroism. We know, too, that he fell, desperately wounded, fighting for the king's cause at Dunkirk. Again the prison gates clanged behind him — this time in 1648 for raising a regiment for the French king. That spoilt child of royalty had a spirit that would not down.

Years before, in 1636, he had had one stroke of good fortune. Let that fertile source of information, Anthony à Wood, again tell the story: " When the King and Queen were for some days entertained at Oxon, he was, at the request of a great Lady belonging to the Queen, made to the Archb. of Cant., then Chancellor of the University, actually created, among other persons of Quality, Master of Arts, tho' but of two years' standing; at which time his conversation being made public, and consequently his ingenuity and generous soul discovered, he became as much admired by the male as before by the female sex." [5]   But all this had happened years before, and things had changed sadly since the former days. All his life he had served the royal cause, and what was his reward? Only the memory of a service well done. He had now become " very poor in body and purse, was the object of charity, went in ragged clothes, and mostly lodged in obscure and dirty places." [6]   Thus courtiers of bonnie King Charlie's reign lived and ended; when Fortune smiled they drank the cup of life deeply, and, when Fortune

[5] *Athenae Oxonienses*, Vol. II, p. 228.
[6] Anthony à Wood, *Athenae Oxonienses*, Vol. II, p. 228.

frowned, drained the cup of death just as deeply.
Now, tradition tells another story of Sir Richard's woes. The beloved "Lucasta" of his many
a poem, known among men as Lucy Sacheverell, was
betrothed to him; but war called him away, cruel
rumor reported him dead at Dunkirk, and Lucasta
hastily married another. "He soon returned to his
native land, imprecated divers anathemas on the sex,
and declined into a vagabond — dying perhaps of
a malady common enough in dark ages, but now
happily banished from genteel society — a broken
heart." [7] Some microscopic critics of to-day doubt
whether Lucasta ever existed outside of Sir Richard's imagination; but they are heartless wretches,
prosaic enough to find " sermons in books and rocks
in running streams." Be that as it may, the story
goes that poor Dick Lovelace — no longer Sir Richard, if you please — spent his greasy shilling in
riotous drinking, and crept down dark, crumbling
stairs to snore on a plank. Then came consumption,
and the story is finished. He was buried in St.
Bride's Church, Fleet Street, but the old building
was destroyed by the Great Fire of 1666, so that
not even his bones exist to-day. And Lucasta —
oh, doubtless she had forgotten him long before!
Yet, luckily, some day

> " Above the highest sphere we meet,
>   Unseen, unknown, and greet as angels greet."

[7] Edwin Whipple, *Authors in their Relation to Life*, p. 32.

Edmund Gosse declares that Lovelace is the most overestimated of the Royalist lyrists,[8] while Lowell says it is "worth while, perhaps, to reprint Lovelace if only to show what dull verses may be written by a man who has made one lucky hit." [9]   Doubtless there is just ground for such opinions.   His days were too full of blood-rousing events to allow him time to perfect his lines.   He wrote hurriedly and never allowed rhyme and rhythm to delay him by any of their insignificant demands.   Both went by the board when they interrupted the undaunted progress of his marvelous conceits.   And what conceits!   Ellinda's glove is a snowy farm with five tenants — all of which is not very flattering to the size of dainty Ellinda's hand.   He goes daily to this farm to pay his rent, five kisses, one for each tenant (doubtless Ellinda had lost her other hand by careless use of some farm implement), and he always finds her out in the meadow picking *hearts!* Without warning the scene changes.   Ellinda's glove is a cabinet, and she will soon come home to it, as any other inhabitant would find the house too small.   Scene three: Ellinda has now become a lute which he cannot master, but he may at least drum upon the case!   Doubtless a little later Ellinda becomes a nebulous angel or an invisible zephyr; but, further, deponent saith not.

If, however, all this pleased Ellinda, why should we rail?   These Cavaliers lived for the day and the

8 Ward's *English Poets,* Vol. II, p. 181.
9 *Library of Old Authors,* Riverside ed., Vol. I, p. 254.

day only.   Little idea had they that posterity would
view their effusions, and if they were not exactly
sceptical as to a heavenly immortality, they were at
least extremely cynical concerning an earthly one.
Therefore Lovelace wrote for a small and temporary audience, consisting of Lucasta and a few
knights, and if these were pleased, he was satisfied.

His was a peculiar temperament.   It may be
true, as he declares, that

> " Stone walls do not a prison make,
>   Nor iron bars a cage,"

but undoubtedly the best poetry has been written
in the open air.   Yet, there is in the better lines of
his songs a certain heroic note that perhaps only
the prison walls could give.   " In prison his poetry
was freer than when he himself was at liberty.   The
fetters on his body seemed not only not to chain his
mind, but to leave it more elastic and buoyant to
roam in the fairy-land of love and poetry . . .
When in the stone walls of his cell he lifts up his
voice and sings in honor of love, of constancy, of
loyalty and truth, he strikes a chord so true, so national, and so universal that we cheerfully lend him
our ears; willingly give ourselves up to the delight
of his verse; and yield him our earnest praise." [10]
It required a brave man to stand at the barred window and stoutly declare to the hostile world that
while he is singing thus the majesty of his king,

[10] Langford, *Prison Books and Their Authors*, p. 212.

" Enlargèd winds, that curl the flood,
    Know no such liberty."

Then, too, those sturdy, gentle lines to Lucasta, as
he marched away to war, may have been sung to an
imaginary " fair lady ", but the sentiment remains
the courageous expression of a high soul:

" I could not love thee, dear, so much
    Loved I not honor more."

" We know that in his two famous lyrics [*To Lucasta, on Going to the Wars* and *To Althea from
Prison*] we possess the real and perfect fruit, the
golden harvest of that troubled and many-sided existence." [11]

Little we have of Sir Richard's that will survive
the jealousy of Time. His comedy, *The Scholar*
(1634), and his tragedy, *The Soldier* (1640), were
lost almost before he himself was, and to this day
no trace of them has been discovered. His *Lucasta:
Epodes, Odes, Sonnets, and Songs* he sent forth from
prison to be published in 1649, and his brother com-
piled the *Posthume Poems* in 1659. But by only a
dozen, at most, of these verses will his name be remembered. And yet what is the difference? How
few, how very few, of the world's very greatest singers are remembered by more! Sir Richard Lovelace begged not for a poet's fame; he asked simply
a loyal courtier's reward, and, failing this, passed
on. Time has been unkind to him; but it matters
not, since he sleeps well.

[11] Repplier, *English Love-Songs, Points of View*, p. 41.

"But ah! the sickle! Golden ears are cropped;
   Ceres and Bacchus bid good night;
Sharp frosty fingers all your flowers have topped,
   And what scythes spared, winds shave off quite."

ABRAHAM COWLEY

(1618 — 1667)

Pope says that he — this highly moral fellow Cowley — got drunk one evening and lay out under a hedge-row all night with a bacchanalian parson, Dean Sprat, and thus caught a fever which carried him off — we are not certain where. But Pope was a spiteful little hunchback and may have invented the tale. Dean Sprat, who was snoring under the hedge-row that night, and who, of course, ought to know, says his friend caught the fever through staying in the hot harvest-field too long. Be that as it may, he died in the year 1667, and since has become almost as dead poetically as he is physically. Long years ago Pope asked,

> "Who now reads Cowley?   If he pleases yet,
> His moral phrase, not his pointed wit;
> Forgot his epic, nay, Pindaric art," [1]

and the same answer would have to be given in these latter days.

It is a rather poor ending for the most famous poet of the seventeenth century — the bard who was considered far greater than Milton, one equalled only by the greatest singers of ancient Greece and Rome, one whom Congreve dubbed " our English

[1] *Epistle to Augustus.*

Horace." [2]   No praise was too high for him in
those old days.   " The darling of my youth," declares
Dryden,[3] and again, " His authority is almost sacred
to me." [4]   Even as modern a poet as Cowper wrote
that he studied, prized, and wished that he had
known, the ingenious Cowley.   But as the years
passed his fame languished, and when such a writer
as Charles Lamb said that, though now out of fashion, he was still a lovable poet, the expression might
have caused surprise, but no sympathetic response.

He really must have been a lovable man — this
Abraham Cowley.   Leigh Hunt declares he " could
not have hurt a fly," [5] and the whole tenor of his
life shows him to have been a kindly, though reserved, Royalist, speaking but little harm against
others and meaning no injury to any save enemies
of the king.   He was — what was rare among those
courtiers — very much a self-made man ; he won his
way not by noble blood, but by sheer genius.
Cowley's father, who died before the boy's birth,
kept a stationer's shop, or, as some would have put
it, a grocery, and there, in the Cheapside section of
London, the boy came into this world and found
himself heir to one hundred and forty pounds left
by the departed parent.   It was not much to start
on ; but his wits stood him in good stead, and we
find him at an early age surprising the masters of
Westminster School with his precocity.   As a mere

2 *The Old Bachelor*, Act IV, Sc. 9.
3 *Essay on Satire.*
4 *Essay on Heroic Plays.*
5 *The Town*, p. 116.

child he had found in his mother's parlor a copy of Spenser's *Faerie Queen,* and the " poet's poet " had aroused in him not only a genuine love of literature, but at the same time a most ardent desire to compose verses of his own. His teachers complained that the boy could never remember the rules of grammar (what natural boy ever could?) ; but when the pedagogues saw what pretty poems he could invent, they said it mattered not, and wisely allowed the question of syntax to pass. Even at that age he was considered a genius in the making. Tradition says that when one of the young masters punished the youngster for writing his name with a burnt stick upon the newly white-washed ceiling of the schoolroom, the head-master threatened to discharge the teacher, commanded that the name remain, and prophesied that little Abraham Cowley would some day be a great man and an honor to the school. 'And so he was, as we shall see.

In his fifteenth year (1633) the boy brought out a volume of five poems, *Poetical Blossoms,* and very good blossoms they were, too — far better than some fruit that resulted from them. Hear just a stanza from the second edition :

" This only grant me, that my means may lie
Too low for envy, for contempt too high.
  Some honor I would have
Not from great deeds, but good alone:
Th' unknown are better than the ill-known;
  Rumor can ope the grave.
'Acquaintance I would have, but when't depends
Not on the number, but the choice of friends."

This second edition, with an added portion called *Sylvia*, appeared in 1636, and a third edition in 1637. Thus, at eighteen he had had better fortune than most poets at fifty. Some of these efforts had been written at a surprisingly early age — *Constantius and Philetus* at twelve and *Pyramus and Thisbe* at ten. And yet how really excellent they are! "After more than two hundred years," says Edmund Gosse, speaking of *Pyramus and Thisbe*, "it remains still readable." [6] The story goes right along with a childlike simplicity, and one cannot help contrasting with it his later more brilliant but laboriously elongated compositions.

The child is father of the man, and so we find it in the life of this quiet, meditative poet. "When I was a very young boy at school," says he, "instead of running about on holidays and playing with my fellows, I was wont to steal from them and walk into the fields, either alone with a book or with some one companion, if I could find any of the same temper." [7] His was just such a nature. He cared little for the glare and tinsel of the court and seemed never to desire to display himself. Wonderful to relate, during his whole life "he never willingly recited any of his writings." [8] Alas, that there are not more Cowleys!

But, quiet, modest, widely-read student that he was, he failed in the examination for election to Cambridge in 1636 and had to wait until June,

[6] *Seventeenth Century Studies*, p. 174.
[7] Cowley's *Of Myself*.
[8] Sprat's *Introduction, Cowley's Poems*.

1637, before he could enter the ancient halls of Trinity. Those obstreperous rules in grammar doubtless hindered him. There at Trinity, however, according to his hedge-row companion, Dr. Sprat, his wit " was both early-ripe and lasting," while he continually surprised the new masters, as he had the old at Westminster, by his wide reading and ability in composition. In 1638 he brought out his pastoral drama, *Love's Riddle*, written, he declares, when he was but sixteen, and in February, 1638, a Latin comedy of his was played with great éclat by the students of Trinity. All this, be it remembered, before his twentieth birthday. During the next year he received his B. A. and in 1642 his M. A.

It was just the year before the latter event that he so happily attracted the notice of Prince Charles by writing *extempore* a comedy, *The Guardian*, and having it acted during the prince's brief visit to Cambridge — all within the space of forty-eight hours. It was a pretty good piece of work, too — so good, in fact, that in spite of Puritan watchfulness it was often acted in private, and was printed in 1650 without the consent of Cowley, who was then in France. In 1658 he rewrote it, called it *The Cutter of Coleman Street*, had it played at Lincoln's Inn Fields in December, 1661, and brought down a hornet's nest about his ears by inserting some expressions that were considered attacks upon the king's party. Cowley, who was never a coward, wrote a straightforward defense of himself and reminded the people of his long service to the king.

But what is the use of arguing with the public?
It is not surprising that he exclaimed in the preface
to the famous play: " If I had a son inclined by
nature to the same folly [poetry], I believe I should
bind him from it by the strictest conjurations of a
paternal blessing. For what can be more ridiculous
than to labor to give men delight, whilst they labor,
on their part, most earnestly to take offense?"

One may well marvel at the precocity of this college boy. Besides the poetry already mentioned,
the Latin comedy, *The Guardian*, and much prose,
he wrote while still a minor, as he and several of his
friends declare, the greater part of the four weighty
books of his epic, *Davideis*. How vast are the
plans of youth! This twenty-year-old poet had in
mind to sing " the barbarous cruelty of Saul to the
priests at Nob, the several flights and escapes of
David, with the manner of his living in the wilder-
ness, the funeral of Samuel, the love of Abigail, the
sacking of Ziglag, the loss and recovery of David's
wives from the Amalekites, the witch of Endor, the
war with the Philistines, and the battle of Gilboa;
all of which I meant to interweave upon several occasions with most of the illustrious stories of the
Old Testament, and to embellish with the most remarkable antiquities of the Jews, and of other nations before or at that Age." [9] Fortunately, the
ambitious bard's enthusiasm had all leaked away by
the time the fourth book was finished; and it is well.
Go, attempt the task of reading one book!

[9] Cowley's *Preface, Poems.*

Cowley undoubtedly had the courage of his convictions, and it is evident that he expressed his opinions plainly. In 1643 he was ejected from Cambridge for holding royalist views, and we next find him at St. John's College, Oxford, where Crashaw and many another follower of gay and deceitful King Charles had gathered. How the old walls of Oxford echoed with merriment and brave oaths! What boasting declarations of loyalty and daring bloodthirstiness were shouted over the wine-glasses! Cowley, in his enthusiasm, wrote *The Puritan and the Papist*, and damned them both. Just here was the tide in his affairs. Having written a touching elegy on the death of a certain Mr. Harvey, he gained the zealous friendship of John Harvey, a brother of the eulogized corpse, and was thus introduced to such lofty gentlemen as Lord St. Albans and the mighty Lord Falkland. He entered into the service of St. Albans, lived with that noble's family, took part in the campaigns about Oxford, continued his studies at St. John's between fights, and capped the climax by attending the queen in her flight to France. Not at all bad for the grocer's son!

Whatever advance, however, Cowley made in the social scale he paid for with many a hard day's work. For twelve laborious years he was absent from England making secret and dangerous journeys into Scotland, Flanders, and Holland, constantly ciphering and deciphering the heavy correspondence between the king and the queen and the loyal statesmen of the times, working often from early morning until far into the night, having little time for meditation and poetry. 'And yet, while an overworked exile, he found time to publish in London, in 1647, *The Mistress* — and how lovers of those old days gloated over it!

> " I never yet could see that face
>   Which had no dart for me;
> From fifteen years to fifty's space,
>   They all victorious be.
> Love, thou'rt a devil, if I may call thee *one;*
> For sure in me thy name is Legion."

When we consider the activities of his life, the many trials and vicissitudes, the constant round of unromantic business, we may well wonder, not that he is sometimes unpoetic, but that he wrote poetry at all.

The time of change, however, was approaching. Sent in 1656 into England to observe conditions there, he suddenly found himself a captive in London — a captive among the most merciless " Christians " the world has ever known. But a good friend paid his bail of a thousand pounds, and he went forth pledged to sin no more — that is, to help no longer his beloved king and queen. Faithfully, it seems, he kept his promise; but that he was weary of this life of anxiety is evidenced by his avowed intention that year of departing for America, " to forsake this world forever, with all the vanities and vexations of it." On his first tour of secret investigation in England he had started the rumor that he was tired of political life and was going to devote his time to the study of medicine. He retired into Kent, and went poking about through the woods and meadows, gathering " simples " and really making some study of their curative properties, and thus so impressed observers that by order of the government he was created an M. D. by Oxford in 1657.   But to Cowley poetry was far dearer than science, and the next year we hear him singing in rhyme and rhythm *the virtues of plants*. The song was six books long, and in Latin at that! The seventeenth century was a very patient, long-suffering age.

After all, though, life must have been rather dreary just then for the poetic doctor.   He had no lady-love, as did the other Cavaliers, to console him; he had loved but once, and then the girl, it seems, had married Dean Sprat's brother.   He wrote love poems, it is true; but hear his own words concerning the sincerity of such songs: " It is not in this sense that poesie is said to be a kind of painting; it is not the picture of the poet, but of things and persons imagined by him.   He may be in his own practice and disposition a philosopher, nay, a Stoic, and yet speak sometimes with the softness of an amorous Sappho." [10]   How hard-hearted old Samuel Johnson snorted over this idea — this " dream of a shadow! "   In his opinion the poet who throws himself into a rage over an imaginary sweetheart is a fool.   He " who praises beauty which he never

[10] Cowley's *Preface, Poems.*

saw, complains of jealousy which he never felt, supposes himself sometimes invited and sometimes forsaken, fatigues his fancy and ransacks his memory for images which may exhibit the gaiety of hope or the gloominess of despair, and dresses his imaginary Chloris or Phyllis sometimes in flowers fading as her beauty, and sometimes in gems lasting as her virtues,"— [11] tommyrot, all of it! But, as has been said, Cowley had neither wife nor sweetheart to comfort him, and Puritan England must have been, indeed, a gloomy home for him.

At last the stern Protector could protect no longer; Death called him. Gladly Cowley hastened away to France and joined the joyful Charles. Now, at last, thought the poet, his trials were over. In 1660 he composed his *Ode upon the Blessed Restoration*, and in 1661 his *Vision Concerning His Late Pretended Highness, Cromwell the Wicked; containing a Discourse in Vindication of Him by a pretended Angel, and the Confutation thereof by the Author, Abraham Cowley.* He was now past forty years of age, and tired of the daily warfare. Had he not deserved long years of rest and prosperity? But who can depend on a king? Months passed, aye, years, and still the reward was withheld. Hard days, indeed, were those for the weary Cowley. He asked for the mastership of Savoy; but his request was ignored. His old play, under a new title, was censured, as we have seen, as an attack upon the Royalists. His enemies, in derision, took delight in reciting in his hearing a spiteful bit of doggerel:

[11] Johnson's *Lives of the Poets: Cowley.*

" Savoy — missing Cowley came into the court,
Making apologies for his bad play:
Everyone gave him so good a report,
That Apollo gave heed to all he could say:

" Nor would he have had, 'tis thought, a rebuke,
Unless he had done some notable folly;
Writ verses unjustly in praise of Sam Tuke
Or printed his pitiful Melancholy."

At length, however, the day of payment came.
Through the intercession of St. Albans and the
Duke of Buckingham he came into possession of
some country estates near London; and although
his income at no time exceeded three hundred pounds,
it was sufficient, and one may believe that he gladly
returned to rural peace. Sprat himself believed it;
but Anthony à Wood declares that, " not finding the
preferment conferred upon him which he expected,
while others for their money carried away most
places, he retired discontented into Surrey." And
yet Cowley had cried, in *The Wish:*

" O fields! O woods! when, when shall I be made
The happy tenant of your shade? "

Willingly or unwillingly, he took first a home at
Barn Elms, and afterwards, in April, 1665, at
Chertsea, where " some friends and books, a cheerful heart and innocent conscience were his constant
companions." [12] But life in rural England was
not quite the pleasant dream that he had expected.

[12] Dr. Sprat's *Preface, Cowley's Poems.*

His homes were not healthful; he was plagued with colds and fevers; "and, besides," he wrote in a letter to his friend Sprat, "I can get no money from my tenants, and have my meadows eaten up every night by cattle put in by neighbors." Doubtless his ill health might have been traced to his wine-cellar, for men of those days were daring drinkers. "We suspect from the portraits of Cowley that his blood was not very healthy by nature," says Leigh Hunt, and he then compares him to Thompson, both of them being "fat men, not handsome, very amiable and sociable; no enemies to a bottle; . . . passionately fond of external nature, of fields, woods, gardens, etc.; bachelors — in love, and disappointed; . . . childlike in their ways." [13] And, strange to say, in those later days he — a Cavalier — would leave the room if a woman entered!

If, however, in his last years he grew more sickly and more cold-blooded, he at least found something of living interest in the vigorous scientific movements of his day. He was one of the first and most zealous members of the Royal Society, and in his once widely read ode to this institution seized the opportunity to praise the greatest scientist of the age — Lord Bacon:

> " From these and all long errors of the way,
> In which our wandering predecessors went,
> And like th' old Hebrews many years did stray
> In deserts but of small extent,
> Bacon, like Moses, led us forth at last.

[13] *Men, Women, and Books*, Vol. II, p. 50.

> The barren wilderness he past
> Did on the very border stand
> Of the blest promis'd land,
> And from the mountain's top of his exalted wit
> Saw it himself, and shew'd us it."

He observed closely the experiments of the learned,
wrote out a plan for a philosophical college, and
composed a most appreciative ode to the deep
thinker, Hobbes:

> " Thou great Columbus of the golden land of new
>   philosophies!
> Thy task was harder much than his,
> For thy learn'd America is
> Not only found out first by thee,
> And rudely left to future industry,
> But thy eloquence and thy wit
> Has planted, peopled, built, and civiliz'd it."

Thus in comparative peace and rest he passed
his last years in the country home at Chertsea.
" It was a little house, with ample gardens and
pleasant meadows attached. Not of brick, indeed, but half timber, with a fine old oak staircase
and balusters and one or two wainscoted chambers,
which yet remain much as when Cowley dwelt there,
as do also the poet's study, a small closet with a
view meadowward to St. Anne's Hill, and the room
overlooking the road, in which he died." [14]   There
he died July 28, 1667, and even busy London
stopped an hour to mourn the loss of a great man.
His corpse, says Evelyn, " lay at Wallingford House,

[14] Thorne, *Hand-Book to the Environs of London.*

and was thence conveyed to Westminster Abbey in
a hearse with six horses and all funeral decency,
near a hundred coaches of noblemen and persons
of quality following; among these all the wits of
the town, divers bishops and clergymen." [15]   And
King Charles turned to his courtiers and said,
" Cowley has not left a better man behind him in
England." He sleeps between Chaucer and Spenser.

This is worthy company; in the opinion of his
day, however, Cowley not only deserved but honored
it. There is always about him and his work a certain gentility, an aristocracy of intellect, if not of
blood. But just here is the trouble with Cowley:
there is too much intellect and not enough of rich
red blood. The man who could deliberately write
six books of rhyme on vegetation, imitating Ovid in
the first two, Catullus in the next two, and Virgil's
Georgics in the last two, was about as capable of
soul-stirring passions as an iceberg. That he was
talented cannot be doubted; but, as Elizabeth Barrett Browning has said, he had " the intellect only
of a great poet, not the sensibility," and did " all
but make us love and weep." [16]   He could not write
a poem without seeming to say, " Lo, how learned I
am!" How many an otherwise excellent line he has
marred with far-away allusions to remote sciences
and philosophies. And what conceits! Samuel
Johnson has pointed the finger of scorn at a multitude of them: for instance, the group in *Knowledge*:

[15] *Diary, August 3, 1667.*
[16] *The Book of the Poets.*

" The sacred tree midst the fair orchard grew;
    The phoenix truth did on it rest,
    And built his perfum'd nest.
That right Porphyrian tree which did true logic show,
    Each leaf did learned notions give,
    And the apples were demonstrations:
So clear their colour and divine,
The very shade they cast did other lights out-shine."

Perhaps in this day of national struggle with mo-
nopolies this couplet in praise of Lord Falkland will
be of interest:

" How could he answer't, if the State saw fit
   To question a monopoly of wit? "

And hear this comment upon a man who has become
so learned that his heart is ossified and can no longer
understand love's ways:

" Another from my mistress' door
    Saw me with eyes all watery come;
Nor could the hidden cause explore,
    But thought some smoke was in the room:—
Such ignorance from unwounded learning came;
He knew tears made by smoke, but not by flame."

Such is Cowley's idea of a love lyric. Ward declares that once famous collection of amorous
songs, *The Mistress*, a complete failure. " Nothing
of what we require of love poetry is there — neither
grace nor glow nor tenderness nor truth. The
passion is neither deeply felt nor lightly uttered." [17]

[17] *English Poets*, Vol. II, p. 238.

Johnson and Addison [18] have so frankly and keenly
laid bare the rhetorical sins of Cowley that there
is little to do save repeat some of the verses pointed
out by these two critics. An " enormous and dis-
gusting hyperbole," says Johnson of this:

" By every wind that comes this way,
　　Send me at least a sigh or two,
　Such and so many I'll repay,
　　As shall themselves make winds to get to you."

And we do not wonder that Samuel's wrath was
aroused by lines such as these:

　　" In tears I'll waste these eyes,
　　　By love so vainly fed;
　　　So lust of old the Deluge punished."
　　and
　　　" Cordials of pity give me now,
　　　　For I too weak for purgings grow."

And, remember, such words to his dainty sweetheart!
How he could cling to a conceit, fondle it, pet it,
and thoroughly spoil it!

Well may Johnson think that no man who has
ever really loved will commend such poetry. Well
may he declare: " The compositions are such as
might have been written for penance by a hermit,
or for hire by a philosophical rhymer who had only
heard of another sex." [19]　And Dryden, in consid-
ering the strained ingenuity of the man, has said:

[18] *Spectator, 62.*
[19] *Lives of the Poets.*

" Donne perplexes the minds of the fair sex with nice speculations of philosophy when he should engage their hearts and entertain them with the softness of love. *In this Mr. Cowley has copied him to a fault.*" [20] In short, Cowley's is about the frostiest love poetry in the English language; it gives forth a cold, hard glitter that could not possibly attract any but an Arctic belle. As Addison says:

> " One glittering thought no sooner strikes our eyes
> With silent wonder, but new wonders rise;
> As in the milky-way a shining white
> O'erflows the heavens with one continued light,
> That not a single star can show his rays." [21]

If, however, we would see really startling figures, bold-prancing, rough-shod metaphors and similes, we must peep into that invention of Cowley's, the Pindaric Ode. In *The Muse*, for instance, Nature is the postilion, Art the coachman, and figures conceits, raptures, love, truth, and " useful lies " strut in livery! And yet this is the poet who, according to Dean Sprat, never runs his readers or his argument out of breath! In the *Davideis* the slightest scriptural hint gives him a chance for a score of descriptive lines, with numerous theological views, philosophical side-glances and biographical winks; and in the meanwhile the leading character humbly sits by the roadside and patiently waits his cue. Epic heroes have ever been noted for their endurance and forbearance.

[20] *Discourse Concerning the Origin and Progress of Satire.*
[21] Addison's *Account of the Greatest English Poets.*

But, after all the drubbings inflicted by Dryden, Addison, and Johnson, there remains in Cowley a good deal that is of genuine worth. If he cannot always write good poetry, he can at least see everything in the poetical light. In spite of the fact that he refuses to view things as a whole, but must forever be dividing them into atoms, in spite of the fact that often you cannot see the house for the ornaments, there are many vigorous and original lines scattered through his works. He is nothing if not original; but it is originality wasted on wrong ideals. He strains for effects, and to us of to-day these effects are nothing short of ludicrous; and yet his age expected them of him and applauded them loudly. That keen critic, Professor Thomas H. Ward, may be partly right when he says: " It is as though in the course of a hundred years the worst fancies which Wyatt had borrowed from Petrarch had become fossilized, and were yet brought out by Cowley to do duty for living thoughts "; [22] but there is a certain simple-minded earnestness in the man's efforts that is a very saving grace. The reader who is at all sympathetic will be inclined to agree with Thomas Campbell that there is always something in Cowley which reminds us of childhood.[23]

His *Anacreontiques* are, to this day, for the most part, rather pleasant reading, and bid fair to live; for " men have been wise in very different modes, but they have always laughed the same way." [24]

[22] *English Poets*, Vol. II, p. 237.
[23] *Specimen of the British Poets.*
[24] Johnson, *Lives of the Poets: Cowley.*

These bits of verse appeal to us, therefore, because of the decidedly " human " strain in them. What a pardonable, even if flimsy, argument is that in *Drinking* — a poem, by the way, that is likely to outlive all else written by Cowley.

Now, too, some of Cowley's odes, in spite of Walt Whitman-like lines, have a sonorousness seldom found among these high-keyed Cavaliers. Read aloud the one to the Royal Society; speak solemnly the lines to his well-loved Crashaw; use your best bass on the ode to the admired Hobbes, and you will be surprised at their dignity and harmony. Nor did he lack imagination; his tortured figures of speech lift appealing hands to heaven in proof of it. Observe Cain destroy his brother;

> " I saw him fling the stone, as if he meant
> At once his murder and his monument." [25]

As Dryden has pointed out, this critic-damned Cowley, in seeking his conceits, " swept, like a drag-net, great and small; " but did he not use the captured minnows in a decidedly original way? He may have lacked judgment, but he did his own thinking, and that is more than the majority of the seventeenth-century poets did. How wrong is the flash-fire Frenchman Taine in declaring that Cowley " possesses all the capacity to say whatever pleases him — but he has just nothing to say." He has a great deal to say — perhaps too much — and he speaks frequently with sincerity, a certain high

[25] *Davideis, Book I.*

quality of moral purity, and even at times with a pleasing poetical cadence.

Sidney Lanier once said that the trouble with Poe was he did not know enough. Perhaps the same critic would have said of Cowley that he knew too much. The man was over-blessed with " wit." Book-learning and an easy pen have never made a poet. For a college may train a man to scan Virgil, make a suspension-bridge, or govern a nation; but it will never create in him the ability to write a soul-lifting poem. Just so with Cowley. One might write on that grave in Westminster Abbey: *Here lies Abraham Cowley. He was broad in his intellect, and sincere in his efforts, but he lacked a heart; therefore men have forgotten him and hear not his songs.*

CAVALIER SONGS

GEORGE WITHER

(1588-1667)

I

SHALL I, WASTING IN DESPAIR

Shall I, wasting in despair,
Die, because a woman's fair?
Or make pale my cheeks with care,
'Cause another's rosy are?
Be she fairer than the day,
Or the flowery meads in May!
    If she be not so to me,
    What care I how fair she be?

Should my heart be grieved or pined,
'Cause I see a woman kind?
Or a well-disposèd nature
Joinèd with a lovely feature?

WITHER—"Never was there a purer or more honorable
spirit, or one which kept closer to the best it knew."—Arnold,
Ward's English Poets, Vol. II, p. 89. Born, Bentworth,
Hants; educated, Magdalen College, Oxford; studied at Lincoln's Inn, 1615; captain of cavalry under Charles I, 1639;
major in Parliamentary Army, 1642; major-general of forces
in Surrey, 1643; imprisoned frequently for libel; died, London
and buried in Savoy Church.

Be she meeker, kinder than
Turtle dove or pelican!
   If she be not so to me,
   ,What care I how kind she be?

Shall a woman's virtues move
Me to perish for her love?
Or her well-deserving known,
Make me quite forget mine own?
Be she with that goodness blest
,Which may gain her name of best!
   If she be not such to me,
   What care I how good she be?

'Cause her fortune seems too high,
Shall I play the fool, and die?
Those that bear a noble mind,
Where they want of riches find,
Think, " What, with them, they would do
,That, without them, dare to woo!"
   And unless that mind I see,
   ,What care I though great she be?

Great, or good, or kind, or fair,
I will ne'er the more despair!
If she love me (this believe!)
I will die, ere she shall grieve!
If she slight me, when I woo,
I can scorn, and let her go!
   For if she be not for me,
   What care I for whom she be?

I. SHALL I, WASTING IN DESPAIR. " Would that we had one more lyric like the immortal ' Shall I, Wasting in Despair,' for many pages of eclogues and satires."—Schelling, *Elizabethan Lyrics*, p. 34.

II

A ROCKING HYMN

Sweet baby, sleep! what ails my dear,
　What ails my darling thus to cry?
Be still, my child, and lend thine ear
　To hear me sing thy lullaby:
　　My pretty lamb, forbear to weep,
　　Be still, my dear, sweet baby, sleep.

Thou blessed soul, what canst thou fear?
　What thing to thee can mischief do?
Thy God is now thy father dear,
　His holy spouse, thy mother, too:
　　Sweet baby, then forbear to weep,
　　Be still, my babe, sweet baby, sleep.

Though thy conception was in sin,
　A sacred bathing thou hast had;
And, though thy birth unclean hath been,
　A blameless babe thou now art made:
　　Sweet baby, then forbear to weep,
　　Be still, my dear, sweet baby, sleep.

II. A ROCKING HYMN. Wither gives the following reason
for writing the hymn: "Nurses usually sing their children
asleep, and through want of pertinent matter, they oft make
use of unprofitable (if not worse) songs. This was therefore
prepared that it might help acquaint them and their nurse-
children with the loving care and kindness of their Heavenly
Father." This devout spirit became so intense that his later
work was marred by his theory that beauty in poetry and in
other arts was a deceitful snare.

Whilst thus thy lullaby I sing,
For thee great blessings ripening be;
Thine eldest brother is a king,
And hath a kingdom bought for thee:
Sweet baby, then forbear to weep,
Be still, my babe, sweet baby, sleep.

Sweet baby, sleep and nothing fear,
For whosoever thee offends,
By thy protector threat'ned are,
And God and angels are thy friends:
Sweet baby, then forbear to weep,
Be still, my babe, sweet baby, sleep.

When God with us was dwelling here,
In little babes he took delight;
Such innocents as thou, my dear,
Are ever precious in his sight:
Sweet baby, then forbear to weep,
Be still, my babe, sweet baby, sleep.

A little infant once was he,
And, strength in weakness, then was laid
Upon his virgin-mother's knee,
That power to thee might be conveyed:
Sweet baby, then forbear to weep,
Be still, my babe, sweet baby, sleep.

In this, thy frailty and thy need,
He friends and helpers doth prepare,
Which thee shall cherish, clothe, and feed,
For of thy weal they tender are:
Sweet baby, then forbear to weep,
Be still, my babe, sweet baby, sleep.

The king of kings, when he was born,
  Had not so much for outward ease;
By Him such dressings were not worn,
  Nor such like swaddling-clothes as these:
    Sweet baby, then forbear to weep,
    Be still, my babe, sweet baby, sleep.

Within a manger lodged thy Lord
  Where oxen lay and asses fed;
Warm rooms we do to thee afford,
  An easy cradle or a bed:
    Sweet baby, then forbear to weep,
    Be still, my babe, sweet baby, sleep.

The wants that he did then sustain
  Have purchased wealth, my babe, for thee;
And by his torments and his pain
  Thy rest and ease secured be:
    My baby, then forbear to weep,
    Be still, my babe, sweet baby, sleep.

Thou hast (yet more) to perfect this
  A promise and an earnest got
Of gaining everlasting bliss,
  Though thou, my babe, perceiv'st it not:
    Sweet baby, then forbear to weep,
    Be still, my babe, sweet baby, sleep.

III

OLD AGE

As this my carnal robe grows old
Soil'd, rent, and worn by length of years,
Let me on that by faith lay hold
Which man in life immortal wears:
    So sanctify my days behind,
    So let my manners be refined,
That when my soul and flesh must part,
There lurk no terrors in my heart.

So shall my rest be safe and sweet
When I am lodgèd in my grave;
And when my soul and body meet,
A joyful meeting they shall have;
    Their essence then shall be divine,
    This muddy flesh shall starlike shine,
And God shall that fresh youth restore
Which will abide for evermore.

ROBERT HERRICK

(1591-1674)

I

TO THE VIRGINS

Gather ye rose-buds while ye may,
  Old time is still a-flying;
And this same flower that smiles to-day,
  To-morrow will be dying.

The glorious lamp of heaven, the sun,
  The higher he's a-getting,
The sooner will his race be run,
  And nearer he's to setting.

That age is best which is the first,
  When youth and blood are warmer;
But being spent, the worse, and worst
  Times still succeed the former.

Then be not coy, but use your time,
  And, while ye may, go marry;
For having lost but once your prime,
  You may forever tarry.

I. To THE VIRGINS. This lyric was set to music by the English composer, Lawes, and enjoyed great popularity during Herrick's day.

II

CORINNA'S GOING A-MAYING

Get up, get up for shame, the blooming morn
Upon her wings presents the god unshorn.
    See how Aurora throws her fair
    Fresh-quilted colors through the air!
    Get up, sweet slug-a-bed, and see
    The dew-bespangling herb and tree.
Each flower has wept, and bowed toward the east,
Above an hour since; yet you not drest,
    Nay! not so much as out of bed?
    When all the birds have matins said,
    And sung their thankful hymns; 'tis sin,
    Nay, profanation to keep in,
Whenas a thousand virgins on this day
Spring, sooner than the lark, to fetch in May.

Rise, and put on your foliage, and be seen
To come forth, like the spring-time, fresh and green
    And sweet as Flora. Take no care
    For jewels for your gown or hair;
    Fear not, the leaves will strew
    Gems in abundance upon you;
Besides, the childhood of the day has kept,
Against you come, some orient pearls unwept;
    Come, and receive them while the light
    Hangs on the dew-locks of the night,
    And Titan on the eastern hill
    Retires himself, or else stands still
Till you come forth.   Wash, dress, be brief in praying:
Few beads are best, when once we go a-Maying.

II. "CORINNA'S GOING A-MAYING . . . is one of the
most perfect studies of idealized village life in the language."
—Masterman, *The Age of Milton*, p. 105.
   The god unshorn. Apollo.
   Titan. The sun.

Come, my Corinna, come; and coming mark
How each field turns a street, each street a park
    Made green, and trimmed with trees; see how
    Devotion gives each house a bough
    Or branch; each porch, each door, ere this
    An ark, a tabernacle is,
Made up of white-thorn neatly interwove,
As if here were those cooler shades of love.
    Can such delights be in the street
    And open fields, and we not see't?
    Come, we'll abroad, and let's obey
    The proclamation made for May,
And sin no more, as we have done, by staying;
But, my Corinna, come, let's go a-Maying.

There's not a budding boy or girl, this day,
But is got up and gone to bring in May.
    A deal of youth, ere this, is come
    Back, and with white-thorn laden home.
    Some have dispatched their cakes and cream,
    Before that we have left to dream;
And some have wept, and woo'd, and plighted troth,
And chose their priest, ere we can cast off sloth.
    Many a green-gown has been given;
    Many a kiss, both odd and even;
    Many a glance, too, has been sent
    From out the eye, love's firmament;
Many a jest told of the key's betraying
This night, and locks picked, yet w'are not a-Maying.
Come, let us go, while we are in our prime,
And take the harmless folly of the time.
    We shall grow old apace and die
    Before we know our liberty.

Each porch, each door. Until very recent years every country porch in Devonshire was decorated with boughs on Mayday.

Our life is short, and our days run
As fast away as does the sun,
And as a vapor, or a drop of rain,
Once lost, can ne'er be found again;
So when or you or I are made
A fable, song, or fleeting shade,
All love, all liking, all delight,
Lies drown'd with us in endless night.
Then while time serves, and we are but decaying;
Come, my Corinna, come, let's go a-Maying.

III

TO DIANEME

Sweet, be not proud of those two eyes,
Which, star-like, sparkle in their skies;
Nor be you proud that you can see
All hearts your captives, yours yet free;
Be you not proud of that rich hair,
Which wantons with the love-sick air;
Whenas that ruby which you wear,
Sunk from the tip of your soft ear,
Will last to be a precious stone,
When all your world of beauty's gone.

IV

A HYMN TO LOVE

I will confess
With cheerfulness,
Love is a thing so likes me,
That, let her lay
On me all day,
I'll kiss the hand that strikes me.

IV. *So likes me.* So suits me, so pleases me.

I will not, I
Now blubb'ring cry:
"It, ah! too late repents me
    That I did fall
    To love at all,
Since love so much contents me."

No, no, I'll be
In fetters free;
While others they sit wringing
    Their hands for pain,
    I'll entertain
The wounds of love with singing.

With flowers and wine,
And cakes divine,
To strike me I will tempt thee;
    Which done, no more
    I'll come before
Thee and thine altars empty.

V

CHERRY-RIPE

Cherry-ripe, ripe, ripe, I cry,
Full and fair ones; come and buy:
If so be you ask me where
They do grow? I answer, there
Where my Julia's lips do smile; —

V. *My Julia's lips.* "The essence of her personality lingers
on every page where Herrick sings of her. His verse is heavy
with her spicy perfumes, glittering with her many-colored
jewels, lustrous with the shimmer of her silken petticoats.
Her very shadow, her sighs, distills sweet odors on the air,
and draws him after her, faint with their amorous languor."—
Repplier: *English Love-Song, Point of View,* p. 33.

There's the land, or cherry-isle,
Whose plantations fully show
All the year where cherries grow.

VI

TO ELECTRA

I dare not ask a kiss,
    I dare not beg a smile,
Lest having that, or this,
    I might grow proud the while.

No, no, the utmost share
    Of my desire shall be
Only to kiss that air
    That lately kissèd thee.

VII

UPON JULIA'S CLOTHING

Whenas in silks my Julia goes,
Till then, methinks, how sweetly flows
That liquefaction of her clothes!
Next, when I cast mine eyes, and see
That brave vibration each way free;
O how that glittering taketh me!

VIII

NIGHT PIECE TO JULIA

Her eyes the glow-worm lend thee,
The shooting stars attend thee,
    And the elves also,
    Whose little eyes glow
Like the sparks of fire, befriend thee.

No will-o'-th'-wisp mislight thee;
Nor snake or slow-worm bite thee;
    But on, on thy way,
    Not making a stay,
Since ghost there's none to affright thee.

Let not the dark thee cumber;
What though the moon does slumber?
    The stars of the night
    Will lend thee their light,
Like tapers clear without number.

Then, Julia, let me woo thee,
Thus, thus to come unto me:
    And when I shall meet
    Thy silv'ry feet,
My soul I'll pour into thee.

VIII. *Slow-worm.* A species of lizard, supposed to be
poisonous.

IX

TO ANTHEA

Bid me to live, and I will live
　　Thy protestant to be;
Or bid me love, and I will give
　　A loving heart to thee.

A heart as soft, a heart as kind,
　　A heart as sound and free,
As in the whole world thou canst find,
　　That heart I'll give to thee.

Bid that heart stay and it will stay,
　　To honor thy decree;
Or bid it languish quite away,
　　And 't shall do so for thee.

Bid me to weep, and I will weep,
　　While I have eyes to see;
And having none, yet I will keep
　　A heart to weep for thee.

Bid me despair, and I'll despair,
　　Under that cypress-tree;
Or bid me die, and I will dare
　　E'en death, to die for thee.

Thou art my life, my love, my heart,
　　The very eyes of me,
And hast command of every part
　　To live and die for thee.

IX. *Thy protestant.* One always protesting his love.

X

THE ROCK OF RUBIES

Some ask'd me where the rubies grew:
  And nothing I did say,
But with my finger pointed to
  The lips of Julia.
Some ask'd how pearls did grow, and where;
  Then spoke I to my girl,
To part her lips, and shew me there
  The quarrelets of pearl.

XI

TO PRIMROSES FILLED WITH MORNING DEW.

Why do ye weep, sweet babes?   Can tears
    Speak grief in you,
    Who were but born
  Just as the modest morn
    Teemed her refreshing dew?
Alas, you have not known that shower
    That mars a flower,
    Nor felt the unkind
  Breath of a blasting wind,
    Nor are ye worn with years,
    Or warped, as we,
    Who think it strange to see
Such pretty flowers, like to orphans young,
To speak by tears before ye have a tongue.
Speak, whimpering younglings, and make known
    The reason why
    Ye droop and weep.

Is it for want of sleep,
Or childish lullaby?
Or that ye have not seen as yet
The violet?
Or brought a kiss
From that sweetheart to this?
No, no, this sorrow shown
By your tears shed
Would have this lecture read:
That things of greatest, so of meanest worth:
Conceived with grief are, and with tears brought forth.

XII

TO DAFFODILS

Fair daffodils, we weep to see
You haste away so soon;
As yet the early rising sun
Has not attained his noon.
Stay, stay,
Until the hasting day
Has run
But to the even-song;
And, having prayed together, we
Will go with you along.
We have short time to stay as you,
We have as short a spring;
As quick a growth to meet decay
As you, or any thing.
We die,
As your hours do, and dry
Away,
Like to the summer's rain;
Or as the pearls of morning's dew,
Ne'er to be found again.

XIII

UPON THE LOSS OF HIS MISTRESSES

I have lost, and lately, these
Many dainty mistresses;
Stately Julia, prime of all;
Sappho next, a principal;
Smooth Anthea, for a skin
White and heaven-like crystalline;
Sweet Electra, and the choice
Myrrha, for the lute and voice.
Next, Corinna, for her wit,
And the graceful use of it;
With Perilla: all are gone,
Only Herrick's left alone,
For to number sorrow by
Their departures hence, and die.

XIV

HIS GRANGE

Though clock,
To tell how night draws hence, I've none,
A cock
I have to sing how day draws on.
I have
A maid, my Prue, by good luck sent,
To save

XIV. *My Prue.* Prudence Baldwin, a most faithful serv-
ant, with Herrick many years. You will note that this oc-
curred in the seventeenth century, not the twentieth.

That little Fates me gave or lent.
      A hen
I keep, which, creaking day by day,
      Tells when
She goes her long white egg to lay.
      A goose
I have, which, with a jealous ear,
      Lets loose
Her tongue to tell what danger's near.
      A lamb
I keep, tame, with my morsels fed,
      Whose dam
An orphan left him, lately dead.
      A cat
I keep, that plays about my house,
      Grown fat
With eating many a miching mouse;
      To these
A Tracy I do keep, whereby
      I please
The more my rural privacy:
      Which are
But toys, to give my heart some ease.
      Where care
None is, slight things do lightly please.

XV

A THANKSGIVING TO GOD

Lord, thou hast given me a cell
      Wherein to dwell,
A little house, whose humble roof
      Is weatherproof,

Miching. Foraging.
A Tracy. His spaniel.

Under the spars of which I lie
    Both soft and dry;
Where thou, my chamber for to ward,
    Hast set a guard
Of harmless thoughts, to watch and keep
    Me while I sleep.
Low is my porch, as is my fate,
    Both void of state;
And yet the threshold of my door
    Is worn by th' poor,
Who thither come and freely get
    Good words or meat.
Like as my parlor, so my hall
    And kitchen's small;
A little buttery, and therein
    A little bin,
Which keeps my little loaf of bread
    Unchipped, unfled;
Some brittle sticks of thorn or briar
    Make me a fire,
Close by whose living coal I sit,
    And glow like it.
Lord, I confess, too, when I dine,
    The pulse is thine,
And all those other bits that be
    There placed by thee;
The worts, the purslane, and the mess
    Of water-cress,
Which of thy kindness thou hast sent;
    And my content
Makes those, and my beloved beet,
    To be more sweet.

XV. *A Thanksgiving to God.* "There is . . . nothing
in English verse to equal the 'Thanksgiving' . . . as an expression of religious trust."— Saintsbury, *History of Elizabethan Literature.* p. 356.
    Unfled. A Shropshire word meaning "not mouldy."

'Tis thou that crown'st my glittering hearth
    With guiltless mirth,
And giv'st me wassail bowls to drink,
    Spiced to the brink.
Lord, 'tis thy plenty-dropping hand
    That soils my land,
And giv'st me, for my bushel sown,
    Twice ten for one;
Thou mak'st my teeming hen to lay
    Her egg each day;
Besides my healthful ewes to bear
    Me twins each year;
The while the conduits of my kine
    Run cream, for wine.
All these, and better, thou dost send
    Me, to this end,
That I should render, for my part,
    A thankful heart,
Which, fired with incense, I resign,
    As wholly thine;
But the acceptance, — that must be,
    My Christ, by thee.

XVI

UPON A MAID

Here she lies, in bed of spice,
Fair as Eve in Paradise;
For her beauty, it was such
Poets could not praise too much.
Virgins, come, and in a ring
Her supremest requiem sing;
Then depart, but see ye tread
Lightly, lightly, o'er the dead.

Wassail bowls. It was formerly the custom to "treat"
neighbors with spiced ale on New Year's eve. In partaking,
the drinkers were supposed to forget old quarrels, and doubtless did, along with everything else.
Soils. Enriches.

XVII

AN ODE FOR BEN JONSON

Ah, Ben!
Say how, or when
Shall we thy guests
Meet at those lyric feasts,
Made at the Sun,
The Dog, the Triple Tun?
Where we such clusters had,
As made us nobly wild, not mad;
And yet each verse of thine
Out-did the meat, out-did the frolic wine.

My Ben!
Or come again:
Or send to us
Thy wit's great over-plus;
But teach us yet
Wisely to husband it;
Lest we that talent spend:
And having once brought to an end
That precious stock, the store
Of such a wit the world should have no more.

XVIII

HIS PRAYER TO BEN JONSON

When I a verse shall make,
Know I have pray'd thee,

XVII. *The Sun, the Dog, the Triple Tun.* Famous London inns of the seventeenth century. The Sun was in Fish Street Hill, the Dog near Whitehall and Westminster Hall, and the Three Tuns in Guildhall Yard. General Monk stayed at the Three Tuns in 1660. All these inns were the evening meeting-places of the gay wits of the century.

For old religion's sake,
  Saint Ben, to aid me.

Make the way smooth for me,
  When I, thy Herrick,
Honouring thee on my knee
  Offer my lyric.

Candles I'll give to thee,
  And a new altar;
And thou, Saint Ben, shalt be
  Writ in my psalter.

XIX

HIS PRAYER FOR ABSOLUTION

For those my unbaptizèd rhymes,
Writ in my wild, unhallowed times,
For every sentence, clause, and word,
That's not inlaid with thee, my Lord,
Forgive me, God, and blot each line
Out of my book that is not thine.
But if, 'mongst all, thou find'st here one
Worthy thy benediction,
That one of all the rest shall be
The glory of my work and me.

XIX. *Prayer for Absolution.* "The jolly, careless Anacreon of the church, with his head and heart crowded with pleasures, threw down at length his wine-cup, tore the roses from his head, and knelt in the dust."— Macdonald: *England's Antiphon*, p. 163.

Wild, unhallowed times. *Cf.* Robert Burns' statement: "A man may live like a fool, but he scarce dies like one."

XX

TO LAURELS

A funeral stone
Or verse, I covet none;
But only crave
Of you that I may have
A sacred laurel springing from my grave;
Which, being seen
Blest with perpetual green,
May grow to be
Not so much called a tree
As the eternal monument of me.

XXI

TO DEATH

Thou bidd'st me come away,
And I'll no longer stay
Than for to shed some tears
For faults of former years,
And to repent some crimes
Done in the present times;
And, next, to take a bit
Of bread, and wine with it;
To don my robes of love,
Fit for the place above;
To gird my loins about
With charity throughout,
And so to travel hence
With feet of innocence:
These done, I'll only cry,
" God, mercy ! " and so die.

XXII

HIS POETRY HIS PILLAR

Only a little more
    I have to write,
        Then I'll give o'er,
And bid the world good-night.

'Tis but a flying minute
    That I must stay,
        Or linger in it;
And then I must away.

O Time, that cut'st down all,
    And scarce leav'st here
        Memorial
Of any men that were!

How many lie forgot
    In vaults beneath,
        And piecemeal rot
Without a fame in death!

Behold this living stone
    I rear for me,
        Ne'er to be thrown
Down, envious Time, by thee.

Pillars let some set up,
    If so they please,
        Here is my hope,
And my pyramides.

XXIII

TO ROBIN RED-BREAST

Laid out for dead, let thy last kindness be
With leaves and moss-work for to cover me;
And while the wood-nymphs my cold corpse inter,
Sing thou my dirge, sweet-warbling chorister!
For epitaph, in foliage, next write this:
Here, here the tomb of Robin Herrick is!

XXIII. *To Robin Red-Breast.* This poem, in its personal
note, its simplicity, its gentleness, its humbleness, its love of
birds and flowers, has a pathos most singular in its appeal.

FRANCIS QUARLES

(1592-1644)

I

MY BELOVED IS MINE

Ev'n like two little bank-dividing brooks,
　That wash the pebbles with their wanton streams,
And having ranged and searched a thousand nooks,
　Meet both at length in silver-breasted Thames,
Where in a greater current they conjoin:
So I my best beloved's am, so he is mine

Ev'n so we met, and, after long pursuit,
　Ev'n so we joined, we both became entire;
No need for either to renew a suit,
　For I was flax and he was flames of fire:
Our firm united souls did more than twine,
So I my best beloved's am, so he is mine.

If all those glitt'ring monarchs that command
　The servile quarters of this earthly ball
Should tender in exchange their shares of land,
　I would not change my fortunes for them all:
Their wealth is but a counter to my coin,
The world's but theirs; but my beloved's mine.

I. *They conjoin . . . he is mine. Conjoin* and *mine*
were good rhymes in the seventeenth century.

180

Nay more, if the fair Thespian ladies all
  Should heap together their diviner treasure,
That treasure should be deemed a price too small
  To buy a minute's lease of half my pleasure:
'Tis not the sacred wealth of all the mine
Can buy my heart from his or his from being mine.

Nor time, nor place, nor chance, nor death can bow
  My least desires unto the least remove;
He's firmly mine by oath, I his by vow;
  He's mine by faith, and I am his by love;
He's mine by water, I am his by wine:
Thus I my best beloved's am, thus he is mine.

He is mine altar, I his holy place;
  I am his guest, and he my living food;
I'm his by penitence, he mine by grace;
  I'm his by purchase, he is mine by blood;
He's my supporting elm and I his vine:
Thus I my best beloved's am; thus he is mine.

He gives me wealth, I give him all my vows;
  I give him songs, he gives me length of days;
With wreaths of grace he crowns my conquering brows,
  And I his temples with a crown of praise;
Which he accepts as an everlasting sign
That I my best beloved's am, that he is mine.

  Thespian ladies. Thespiae, the home of Phryne.

II

SWEET PHOSPHOR, BRING THE DAY

" Lighten mine eyes, O Lord, lest I sleep the sleep of death."—Ps. xiii. 3.

Will 't ne'er be morning? Will that promis'd light
  Ne'er break, and clear these clouds of night?
Sweet Phosphor, bring the day,
  Whose conqu'ring ray
May chase these fogs; sweet Phosphor, bring the
    day.

How long! how long shall these benighted eyes
Languish in shades, like feeble flies
Expecting Spring! How long shall darkness soil
  The face of earth, and thus beguile
The souls of sprightful action; when will day
  Begin to dawn, whose new-born ray
May gild the weathercocks of our devotion,
  And give our unsoul'd souls new motion!
      Sweet Phosphor, bring the day
      Thy light will fray
These horrid mists; sweet Phosphor, bring the day.

Let those have night that silly love t'immure
Their cloister'd crimes, and sin secure;
Let those have night that blush to let men know
  The baseness they ne'er blush to do;
Let those have night that love to take a nap
  And loll in Ignorance's lap;
Let those whose eyes, like owls, abhor the light,
  Let those have night that love the night!
      Sweet Phosphor, bring the day;
      How sad delay
Afflicts dull hopes! sweet Phosphor, bring the day.

Alas! my light-in-vain-expecting eyes
Can find no objects but what rise
From this poor mortal blaze, a dying spark
  Of Vulcan's forge, whose flames are dark
And dangerous, a dull blue-burning light,
  As melancholy as the night:
Here's all the suns that glisten in the sphere
  Of earth: Ah me! what comfort's here?
        Sweet Phosphor, bring the day;
          Haste, haste away
Heav'n's loitering lamp; sweet Phosphor,
          bring the day.

Below, Ignorance: O thou, whose idle knee
Rocks earth into a lethargy,
And with thy sooty fingers hast bedight
  The world's fair cheeks, blow, blow thy spite;
Since thou hast puffed our greater taper, do
Puff on, and out the lesser too;
If e'er that breath-exilèd flame return,
  Thou hast not blown, as it will burn.
        Sweet Phosphor, bring the day;
          Light will repay
The wrongs of night; sweet Phosphor, bring the
    day.

III

O WHITHER SHALL I FLY

O whither shall I fly? What path untrod
Shall I seek out to 'scape the flaming rod
Of my offended, of my angry God?

III. O WHITHER SHALL I FLY? "Oh, that thou wouldest hide me in the grave, that thou wouldest keep me secret, until thy wrath be past, that thou wouldest appoint me a set time, and remember me."—Job, xiv. 13.

Where shall I sojourn? What kind sea will hide
My head from thunder? Where shall I abide,
Until his flames be quenched or laid aside?

What if my feet should take their hasty flight,
And seek protection in the shades of night?
Alas, no shades can blind the God of Light.

What if my soul should take the wings of day,
And find some desert? If she spring away,
The wings of vengeance clip as fast as they.

What if some solid rock should entertain
My frighted soul? Can solid rocks restrain
The stroke of Justice, and not cleave in twain?

Nor sea, nor shade, nor shield, nor rock, nor cave,
Nor silent deserts, nor the sullen grave,
Where flame-eyed Fury means to smite, can save.

The seas will part, graves open, rocks will split,
The shield will cleave, the frighted shadows flit;
Where Justice aims, her fiery darts must hit.

No, no, if stern-browed Vengeance means to thunder,
There is no place above, beneath, nor under,
So close but will unlock or rive in sunder.

'T is vain to flee; 't is neither here nor there
Can 'scape that hand until that hand forbear.
Ah me! where is he not that's everywhere?

'T is vain to flee; till gentle Mercy show
Her better eye, the further off we go,
The swing of Justice deals the mightier blow.

    Clip. Go swiftly.

Th' ingenuous child, corrected, doth not fly
His angry mother's hand, but clings more nigh,
And quenches with his tears her flaming eye.

Shadows are faithless, and the rocks are false;
No trust in brass, no trust in marble walls;
Poor cots are even as safe as princes' halls.

Great God, there is no safety here below;
Thou art my fortress, though thou seemst my foe;
'T is thou that strik'st must guard the blow.

Thou art my God; by thee I fall or stand,
Thy grace hath given me courage to withstand
All tortures, but my conscience and thy hand

I know thy justice is thyself; I know,
Just God, thy very self is mercy, too;
If not to thee, where, whither should. I go?

Then work thy will; if passion bid me flee,
My reason shall obey; my wings shall be
Stretched out no further than from thee to thee.

GEORGE HERBERT

(1593-1633)

I

LOVE

Thou art too hard for me in love;
There is no dealing with thee in that art,
That is thy masterpiece, I see.
When I contrive and plot to prove
Something that may be conquest on my part,
Thou still, Q Lord, outstrippest me.

Sometimes, when as I wash, I say,
And shrewdly as I think, Lord, wash my soul,
More spotted than my flesh can be!
But then there comes into my way
Thy ancient baptism, which when I was foul,
And knew it not, yet cleansèd me.

I took a time when thou didst sleep,
Great waves of trouble combating my breast:
I thought it brave to praise thee then;
Yet then I found that thou didst creep
Into my heart with joy, giving more rest
Than flesh did lend thee back again.

I. Love. "There is something a little feverish and dis-
proportioned in his passionate heart-searchings." — Sincox,
Ward's English Poets, Vol. II, p. 193. It is an interesting
exercise to compare Herbert's religious attitude with that of
Crashaw and of Vaughan.

Let me but once the conquest have
Upon the matter, 'twill thy conquest prove:
If thou subdue mortality,
Thou dost no more than doth the grave;
Whereas if I o'ercome thee and thy love,
Hell, Death, and Devil come short of me.

II

VIRTUE

Sweet day, so cool, so calm, so bright,
  The bridal of the earth and sky;
The dew shall weep thy fall to-night;
  For thou must die.

Sweet rose, whose hue, angry and brave,
  Bids the rash gazer wipe his eye;
Thy root is ever in its grave,
  And thou must die.

Sweet spring, full of sweet days and roses,
  A box where sweets compacted lie;
My music shows ye have your closes,
  And all must die.

Only a sweet and virtuous soul,
  Like seasoned timber, never gives;
But, though the whole world turn to coal,
  Then chiefly lives.

II. *Bridal.* Originally *bride-ale*, meaning the bride's feast.
Doubtless Herbert had this meaning in mind.
  Angry and brave. Anger suggested by red. *Brave* probably means *gaudy*.

III

FRAILTY

Lord, in my silence how do I despise
　　　What upon trust
Is stylèd honor, riches, or fair eyes,
　　　But is fair dust!
　　I surname them gilded clay,
　　Dear earth, fine grass or hay;
In all, I think my foot doth ever tread
　　　Upon their head.

But when I view abroad both regiments,
　　　The world's and thine,
Thine clad with simpleness and sad events,
　　　The other fine,
　　Full of glory and gay weeds,
　　Brave language, braver deeds,
That which was dust before doth quickly rise,
　　　And prick mine eyes.

O brook not this, lest if what even now
　　　My foot did tread
Affront those joys wherewith thou didst endow
　　　And long since wed
　　My poor soul, even sick of love,—
　　It may a Babel prove,
Commodious to conquer heaven and thee,
　　　Planted in me.

IV

EMPLOYMENT

If as a flower doth spread and die,
   Thou wouldst extend me to some good,
Before I were by frost's extremity
      Nipt in the bud;

The sweetness and the praise were thine;
   But the extension and the room
Which in thy garland I should fill, were mine
      At thy great doom.

For as thou dost impart thy grace,
   The greater shall our glory be.
The measure of our joys is in this place,
      The stuff with thee.

Let me not languish, then, and spend
   A life as barren to thy praise
As is the dust, to which that life doth tend,
      But with delays.

All things are busy; only I
   Neither bring honey with the bees,
Nor flowers to make that, nor the husbandry
      To water these.

I am no link of thy great chain,
   But all my company is a weed.
Lord, place me in thy consort; give one strain
      To my poor reed.

IV. *All my company is a weed.* I am an outcast, like the
weed by the roadside.

V

(THE PULLEY

When God at first made man,
Having a glass of blessing standing by;
Let us (said he) pour on him all we can:
Let the world's riches, which dispersed lie,
    Contract into a span.

So strength first made a way;
Then beauty flow'd, then wisdom, honour, pleasure;
When almost all was out, God made a stay,
Perceiving that alone, of all his treasure,
    Rest at the bottom lay.

For if I should (said he)
Bestow this jewel also on my creature,
He would adore my gifts instead of me,
And rest in Nature, not the God of Nature;
    So both should losers be.

Yet let him keep the rest,
But keep them with repining restlessness:
Let him be rich and weary, that, at least,
If goodness lead him not, yet weariness
    May toss him to my breast.

VI

THE QUIP

The merry World did on a day
With his train-bands and mates agree
To meet together where I lay,
And all in sport to jeer at me.

VI. *Train-bands.* Citizen soldiers.

First, Beauty crept into a rose,
Which when I pluckt not, " Sir," said she,
" Tell me, I pray, whose hands are those? "
But thou shalt answer, Lord, for me.

Then Money came, and chinking still,
" What tune is this, poor man? " said he;
" I heard in music you had skill: "
But thou shalt answer, Lord, for me.

Then came brave Glory, puffing by
In silks that whistled, who but he?
He scarce allowed me half an eye:
But thou shalt answer, Lord, for me.

Then came quick Wit and Conversation,
And he would needs a comfort be,
And, to be short, make an oration:
But thou shalt answer, Lord, for me.

Yet when the hour of thy design
To answer these fine things shall come,
Speak not at large, say, I am thine,
And then they have their answer home.

Quick wit. Not humor, but mental ability.

DR. JOHN WILSON

(1595?-1673)

I

LOVE WITH EYES AND HEART

When on mine eyes her eyes first shone.
    I, all amazèd,
    Steadily gazèd,
And she, to make me more amazèd,
So caught, so wove, four eyes in one
As who had with advisement seen us
Would have admired love's equal force between us.

But treason in those friend-like eyes,
    My heart first charming
    And then disarming,
So maimed it, e'er it dreamed of harming,
As at her mercy now it lies,
And shews me, to my endless smart,
She loved but with her eyes, I with my heart.

WILSON. A native of Feversham, Kent; chamber-musician
to Charles I; Doctor of Music, Oxford, 1644; retired to a
country home in Oxfordshire on surrender of Oxford, 1646;
Professor of Music, Oxford, 1656; aroused great interest
among the students by his recitals and lectures; chamber-
musician to Charles II; died, London. He was considered
the best lute player of the century.

II

LOVE'S IDOLATRY

When I behold my mistress' face,
Where beauty hath her dwelling-place,
And see those seeing stars, her eyes,
In whom love's fire for ever lies,
And hear her witty, charming words
Her sweet tongue to mine ear affords,
Methinks he wants wit, ears, and eyes
Whom love makes not idolatrise.

III

THE EXPOSTULATION.

Greedy lover, pause awhile,
And remember that a smile
          Heretofore
Would have made thy hopes a feast;
          Which is more
Since thy diet was increased,
Than both looks and language, too,
Or the face itself, can do.

Such a province is my hand
As, if it thou couldst command
          Heretofore,
There thy lips would seem to dwell;
          Which is more,
Ever since they sped so well,
Than they can be brought to do
By my neck and bosom, too.

II. *Witty.* Full of sense.

If the center of my breast,
A dominion unpossessed
        Heretofore,
May thy wandering thoughts suffice,
        Seek no more,
And my heart shall be thy prize:
So thou keep above the line,
All the hemisphere is thine.

If the flames of love were pure,
Which by oath thou didst assure
        Heretofore,
Gold that goes into the clear
        Shines the more
When it leaves again the fire:
Let not, then, those looks of thine
Blemish what they should refine.

I have cast into the fire
Almost all thou couldst desire
        Heretofore;
But I see thou art to crave
        More and more.
Should I cast in all I have,
So that I were ne'er so free,
Thou wouldst burn, though not for me.

III. *The clear.* The refiner's fire.

THOMAS CAREW

(1598-1639)

I

A SONG

Ask me no more where Jove bestows,
When June is past, the fading rose;
For in your beauty's orient deep
These flowers, as in their causes, sleep.

Ask me no more whither do stray
The golden atoms of the day;
For, in pure love, heaven did prepare
Those powders to enrich your hair.

Ask me no more whither doth haste
The nightingale, when May is past;
For in your sweet dividing throat
She winters, and keeps warm her note.

Ask me no more where those stars light,
That downwards fall in dead of night;
For in your eyes they sit, and there
Fixed become, as in their sphere.

I. Song. "It is the special glory of Carew that he formularized the practice of writing courtly amorous poetry."— Gosse, *Ward's English Poets,* Vol. II, p. 111. For a beautiful appreciation of Carew's work, see the essay by Richard Le Gallienne in *Retrospective Reviews,* II, 80.

Dividing. Playing or singing music with variations (divisions).

Ask me no more if east or west,
The phœnix builds her spicy nest;
For unto you at last she flies,
And in your fragrant bosom dies.

II

MEDIOCRITY REJECTED

Give me more love, or more disdain;
 The torrid, or the frozen zone
Bring equal ease unto my pain;
 The temperate affords me none:
Either extreme, of love or hate,
Is sweeter than a calm estate.

Give me a storm; if it be love,
 Like Danaë in that golden shower
I swim in pleasure; if it prove
 Disdain, that torrent will devour
My vulture-hopes; and he's possessed
Of heaven that's but from hell released.
Then crown my joys, or cure my pain;
Give me more love, or more disdain.

III

PERSUASIONS TO JOY

If the quick spirits in your eye
Now languish, and anon must die;
If every sweet and every grace
Must fly from that forsaken face:
 Then, Celia, let us reap our joys
 Ere time such goodly fruit destroys.

'Or, if that golden fleece must grow
For ever, free from agèd snow;
If those bright suns must know no shade,
Nor your fresh beauties ever fade;
Then fear not, Celia, to bestow
What still, being gathered, still must grow:
    Thus, either Time his sickle brings
    In vain, or else in vain his wings.

IV

TO MY INCONSTANT MISTRESS

When thou, poor excommunicate
    From all the joys of love, shalt see
The full reward and glorious fate
    Which my strong faith shall purchase me,
    Then curse thine own inconstancy.

A fairer hand than thine shall cure
    That heart which thy false oaths did wound;
And to my soul, a soul more pure
    Than thine shall by love's hand be bound,
    And both with equal glory crowned.

Then shalt thou weep, entreat, complain
    To Love, as I did once to thee;
When all thy tears shall be as vain
    As mine were then, for thou shalt be
    Damned for thy false apostasy.

V.

CELIA SINGING

You that think love can convey
No other way
But through the eyes, into the heart
His fatal dart,
Close up those casements, and but hear
This siren sing;
And on the wing
Of her sweet voice it shall appear
That love can enter at the ear.

Then unveil your eyes, behold
The curious mould
Where that voice dwells; and as we know
When the cocks crow
We freely may
Gaze on the day;
So may you, when the music's done,
Awake, and see the rising sun.

VI

IN THE PERSON OF A LADY TO HER INCONSTANT SERVANT

When on the altar of my hand
(Bedewed with many a kiss and tear)
Thy now revolted heart did stand
An humble martyr, thou didst swear

V. CELIA SINGING. *Cf.* Marvell's *The Fair Singer.*

Thus (and the god of love did hear):
" By those bright glances of thine eye,
Unless thou pity me, I die."

When first those perjured lips of thine,
   Bepaled with blasting sighs, did seal
Their violated faith on mine,
   From the soft bosom that did heal
   Thee, thou my melting heart didst steal;
My soul, enflamed with thy false breath,
Poisoned with kisses, sucked in death.

Yet I nor hand nor lip will move,
   Revenge or mercy to procure
From the offended god of love;
   My curse is fatal, and my pure
   Love shall beyond thy scorn endure.
If I implore the gods, they'll find
Thee too ungrateful, me too kind.

VII

IN PRAISE OF HIS MISTRESS

You that will a wonder know,
    Go with me;
Two suns in a heaven of snow
    Both burning be,—
All they fire that do but eye them,
Yet the snow's unmelted by them.

Leaves of crimson tulips met
    Guide the way
Where two pearly rows be set,
    As white as day;

When they part themselves asunder
She breathes oracles of wonder.

'All this but the casket is
    Which contains
Such a jewel, as to miss
    Breeds endless pains,—
That's her mind, and they that know it
May admire, but cannot show it.

VIII

RED AND WHITE ROSES

Read in these roses the sad story
Of my hard fate and your own glory:
In the white you may discover
The paleness of a fainting lover;
In the red, the flames still feeding
On my heart with fresh wounds bleeding.

The white will tell you how I languish,
And the red express my anguish:
The white my innocence displaying,
The red my martyrdom betraying.
The frowns that on your brow resided,
Have those roses thus divided;
O! let your smiles but clear the weather,
And then they both shall grow together.

IX

SONG

Would you know what's soft?   I dare
Not bring you to the down, or air,
Nor to stars to show what's bright,
Nor to snow to teach you white;

Nor, if you would music hear,
Call the orbs to take your ear;
Nor, to please your sense, bring forth
Bruisèd nard, or what's more worth;

Or on food were your thoughts placed,
Bring you nectar for a taste;
Would you have all these in one,
Name my mistress, and 'tis done!

X

MURDERING BEAUTY

I'll gāze no more on that bewitchèd face,
Since ruin harbors there in every place,
For my enchanted soul alike she drowns
With calms and tempests of her smiles and frowns.
I'll love no more those cruel eyes of hers,
Which, pleased or angered, still are murderers;
For if she dart like lightning through the air
Her beams of wrath, she kills me with despair;
If she behold me with a pleasing eye,
I surfeit with excess of joy, and die.

EDMUND WALLER

(1605-1687)

I

GO, LOVELY ROSE

Go, lovely rose,
Tell her that wastes her time and me,
That now she knows,
When I resemble her to thee,
How sweet and fair she seems to be.

Tell her that's young,
And shuns to have her graces spied,
That, had'st thou sprung
In deserts where no men abide,
Thou must have uncommended died.

Small is the worth
Of beauty from the light retired;
Bid her come forth,
Suffer herself to be desired,
And not blush so to be admired.

Then die, that she
The common fate of all things rare
May read in thee:
How small a part of time they share,
That are so wondrous sweet and fair.

I. Go, Lovely Rose. Cf. Waller's *The Bud.* "No man
better understood the art of flattery and how to administer it
with grace."— Scoones, *Four Centuries of English Letters,* p.
95.

II

SONG

Stay, Phoebus, stay!
The world to which you fly so fast,
          Conveying day
From us to them, can pay your haste
With no such object, nor salute your rise
With no such wonder as De Mornay's eyes.

Well does this prove
The error of those antique books
          Which made you move
About the world: her charming looks
Would fix your beams, and make it ever day,
Did not the rolling earth snatch her away.

III

ON THE FRIENDSHIP BETWIXT SACCHARIS-
SA AND AMORET

Tell me, lovely, loving pair,
     Why so kind and so severe?
Why so careless of our care,
     Only to yourselves so dear?

II. *De Mornay.* Thought to have been one of the attend-
ants on Queen Henrietta.
Well does this prove. A rather laborious conceit referring
to the ancient belief that the sun moves around the world.
III. *Saccharissa.* Dorothea Sidney, a daughter of the
Earl of Leicester and grandniece of Sir Philip Sidney. She
became Lady Spencer in 1639, and, of course, Waller ceased
to indite love poems to her. Amoret was probably Lady So-
phia Murray. Saccharissa from *saccharum,* sugar.

By this cunning change of hearts
  You the power of Love control;
While the boy's deluded darts
  Can arrive at neither soul.

For in vain to either breast
  Still beguilèd Love does come,
Where he finds a foreign guest:
  Neither of your hearts at home.

Debtors thus with like design,
  When they never mean to pay,
That they may the law decline,
  To some friend make all away.

Not the silver doves that fly,
  Yoked to Cytherea's car,
Not the wings that lift so high
  And convey her son so far,

Are so lovely, sweet, and fair,
  Or do more ennoble love,
Are so choicely matched a pair,
  Or with more consent do move.

Lovely, sweet and fair. "He lives in her name more than
she does in his poetry; he gave that name a charm and a
celebrity which has survived the admiration his verses inspired, and which has assisted to preserve them and himself
from oblivion."—Jameson, *The Loves of the Poets,* Vol. II,
p. 15.

IV

ON A GIRDLE

That which her slender waist confined
Shall now my joyful temples bind;
No monarch but would give his crown,
His arms might do what this has done.

It was my heaven's extremest sphere,
The pale which held that lovely deer;
My joy, my grief, my hope, my love,
Did all within this circle move.

A narrow compass, and yet there
Dwelt all that's good and all that's fair;
Give me but what this ribband bound,
Take all the rest the sun goes round!

V

TO FLAVIA

'Tis not your beauty can engage
  My wary heart:
The sun, in all his pride and rage,
  Has not that art;
And yet he shines as bright as you,
If brightness could our souls subdue.

IV. ON A GIRDLE. "It is only in detached passages, single stanzas, or small pieces, finished with great care and elegance, as the lines on a lady's girdle, . . . that we can discern that play of fancy, verbal sweetness, and harmony which gave so great a name to Waller for more than a hundred years."—Carruthers, *Encyclopædia Britannica* (1860).

'Tis not the pretty things you say,
  Nor those you write,
Which can make Thyrsis' heart your prey;
  For that delight,
The graces of a well-taught mind,
In some of our own sex we find.

No, Flavia, 't is your love I fear;
  Love's surest darts,
Those which so seldom fail him, are
  Headed with hearts;
Their very shadows make us yield;
Dissemble well, and win the field.

VI

TO PHYLLIS

Phyllis, why should we delay,
Pleasures shorter than the day?
Could we (which we never can)
Stretch our lives beyond their span,
Beauty like a shadow flies,
And our youth before us dies;
Or, would youth a beauty stay,
Love hath wings, and will away.
Love hath swifter wings than Time:
Change in love to heaven does climb;
Gods, that never change their state,
Vary oft their love and hate.
Phyllis, to this truth we owe
All the love betwixt us two.

V. *Thyrsis.* The name applied by Waller to himself during his stately and poetical wooing of Saccharissa.

VI. To PHYLLIS. Set to music in Playford's *Select Airs and Dialogues,* 1659. The poem shows the tendency toward the more restrained poetry coming after the Restoration.

Let not you and I enquire
What has been our past desire;
On what shepherds you have smiled,
Or what nymphs I have beguiled;
Leave it to the planets, too,
What we shall hereafter do:
For the joys we now may prove,
Take advice of present love.

VIı

THE BUD

Lately on yonder swelling bush,
  Big with many a coming rose,
This early bud began to blush
  And did but half itself disclose;
I plucked it, though no better grown,
And now you see how full 'tis blown.

Still as I did the leaves inspire,
  With such a purple light they shone
As if they had been made of fire,
  And spreading so, would flame anon.
All that was meant by air or sun,
To the young flower my breath has done.

If our loose breath so much can do,
  What may the same informed of love,—
Of purest love and music, too,—
  When Flavia it aspires to move;
When that which lifeless buds persuades
To wax more soft, her youth invades?

VIII

OF THE LAST VERSES IN THE BOOK

When we for age could neither read nor write,
The subject made us able to indite;
The soul, with nobler resolutions decked,
The body stooping, does herself erect.
No mortal parts are requisite to raise
Her that, unbodied, can her Maker praise.

The seas are quiet when the winds give o'er;
So, calm we when passions are no more!
For then we know how vain it was to boast
Of fleeting things, so certain to be lost.
Clouds of affection from our younger eyes
Conceal that emptiness which age descries.

The soul's dark cottage, battered and decayed,
Lets in new light through chinks that time has made;
Stronger by weakness, wiser men become,
As they draw near to their eternal home.
Leaving the old, both worlds at once they view,
That stand upon the threshold of the new.

VIII. THE LAST VERSES. Waller's son spoke of these lines
as "the last verses my dear father made." Here we may see
how closely the poet has approached the couplet form, soon
to be used so successfully in the "classical" period.

WILLIAM HABINGTON

(1605-1654)

I

HIS MISTRESS FLOUTED

Fine young folly, though you were
That fair beauty I did swear,
  Yet you ne'er could reach my heart;
For we courtiers learn at school
Only with your sex to fool;
  You're not worth the serious part.

When I sigh and kiss your hand,
Cross my arms and wondering stand,
  Holding parley with your eye,
Then dilate on my desires,
Swear the sun ne'er shot such fires —
  All is but a handsome lie.

HABINGTON. Born of a Catholic family at Hindlip, Worcestershire; educated at St. Omer and Paris; married Lucy Herbert, daughter of Lord Powis; lived at all times a life of extreme purity. "He was considered an accomplished gentleman, especially learned in history; but he did run with the times, and was not unknown to Oliver the Usurper."—Anthony à Wood, *Athenae Oxon.*
  I. HIS MISTRESS FLOUTED. From Habington's play, *Cleodora, the Queen of Arragon*, 1640, presented at Whitehall before the king and the queen.

When I eye your curl or lace,
Gentle soul, you think your face
   Straight some murder doth commit;
And your virtue doth begin
To grow scrupulous of my sin,
   When I talk to show my wit.

Therefore, madam, wear no cloud,
Nor to check my love grow proud;
   In sooth, I much do doubt
'Tis the power in your hair,
Not your breath, perfumes the air,
   And your clothes that set you out.

Yet though truth has this confessed,
And I vow I love in jest,
   When I next begin to court,
And protect an amorous flame,
You will swear I in earnest am.
   Bedlam! this is pretty sport.

II

TO ROSES

In the Bosom of Castara

Ye blushing virgins happy are
In the chaste nunn'ry of her breasts,
For he'd profane so chaste a fair
   Who e'er should call them Cupid's nests.

II. CASTARA. Lady Lucy Herbert, whom he married about
1631. "One of the most elegant monuments ever raised by
genius to conjugal affection was Habington's *Castara*."—
Jameson, *The Loves of the Poets*, Vol. II, p. 110.
   Chaste nunnery. Cf. Lovelace's *To Lucasta, On Going to
the Wars.*

Transplanted thus, how bright ye grow,
How rich a perfume do ye yield!
In some close garden, cowslips so
Are sweeter than i' th' open field.

In those white cloisters live secure
From the rude blasts of wanton breath,
Each hour more innocent and pure,
Till you shall wither into death.

Then that which living gave you room
Your glorious sepulchre shall be.
There wants no marble for a tomb,
Whose breast hath marble been to me.

III

AGAINST THEM THAT LAY UNCHASTITY TO THE SEX OF WOMAN

They meet with but unwholesome springs
And summers which infectious are,
They hear but when the mermaid sings,
And only see the falling star,
    Who ever dare
Affirm no woman chaste and fair.

II. *Close garden.* Enclosed.
III. *Against Them.* A reply to Donne's *Song* containing
the words:
    " Ride ten thousand days and nights
    Till age snow white hairs on thee;
    Thou, when thou return'st wilt tell me
    All strange wonders that befell thee,
        And swear
        No where
    Lives a woman true and fair."

Go, cure your fevers, and you'll say
    The dog-days scorch not all the year;
In copper mines no longer stay,
    But travel to the west and there
        The right ones see,
And grant all gold's not alchemy.

What madman, 'cause the glow-worm's flame
    Is cold, swears there's no warmth in fire?
'Cause some make forfeit of their name
    And slave themselves to man's desire,
        Shall the sex, free
From guilt, damnèd to bondage be?

Nor grieve, Castara, though 'twere frail,
    Thy virtue then would brighter shine,
When thy example should prevail
    And every woman's faith be thine:
        And were there none,
'Tis majesty to rule alone.

IV.

DESCRIPTION OF CASTARA

Like the violet, which alone
Prospers in some happy shade,
My Castara lives unknown,
To no looser eye betrayed,
    For she's to herself untrue
    Who delights i' th' public view.

IV. DESCRIPTION OF CASTARA. "The poet dins the chastity of his mistress into his readers' heads until the readers, in self-defense, are driven to say, 'Sir, did any one doubt it'?"—Saintsbury, *History of Elizabethan Literature*, p. 382.

Such is her beauty as no arts
Have enriched with borrowed grace;
Her high birth no pride imparts,
For she blushes in her place.
    Folly boasts a glorious blood,
    She is noblest, being good.

Cautious, she knew never yet
What a wanton courtship meant;
Nor speaks loud to boast her wit,
In her silence eloquent:
    Of her self survey she takes,
    But 'tween men no difference makes.

She obeys with speedy will
Her grave parents' wise commands;
And so innocent that ill
She nor acts nor understands;
    Women's feet shall run astray
    If once to ill they know the way.

She sails by that rock, the court,
Where oft honour splits her mast,
And retiredness thinks the port
Where her fame may anchor cast:
    Virtue safely cannot sit
    Where vice is enthroned for wit.

She holds that day's pleasure best
Where sin waits not on delight;
Without mask, or bail, or feast,
Sweetly spends a winter's night:
    O'er that darkness, whence is thrust
    Prayer and sleep, oft governs lust.

She her throne makes reason climb,
While wild passions captive lie;
And each article of time
Her pure thoughts to Heaven fly:
All her vows religious be,
And her love she vows to me.

V

NOX NOCTI INDICAT SCIENTIAM

When I survey the bright
Celestial sphere,
So rich with jewels hung that night
Doth like an Ethiop bride appear,

My soul her wings doth spread,
And heavenward flies,
The Almighty's mysteries to read
In the large volume of the skies.

For the bright firmament
Shoots forth no flame
So silent, but is eloquent
In speaking the Creator's name.

No unregarded star
Contracts its light
Into so small a character,
Removed far from our human sight,

V. Nox Nocti Indicat Scientiam. "The heavens declare
the glory of God," etc.—Psalm xix.
My soul her wings. "But they that wait upon the Lord
shall renew their strength; they shall mount up with wings
as eagles; they shall run and not be weary; and they shall
walk, and not faint."— Isaiah, xl. 31.
Bright firmament. "The firmament sheweth His handi-
work."— Psalm xix. 1.

But, if we steadfast look,
    We shall discern
In it, as in some holy book,
How man may heavenly knowledge learn.

It tells the conqueror
    That far stretched power,
Which his proud 1angers traffic for,
Is but the triumpn of an hour.

That from the farthest north
    Some nation may,
Yet undiscovered, issue forth,
And o'er his new-got conquest sway.

Some nation yet shut in
    With hills of ice
May be let out to scourge his sin,
Till they shall equal him in vice.

And then they likewise shall
    Their ruin have;
For as yourselves your empires fall,
And every kingdom hath a grave.

Thus those celestial fires,
    Though seeming mute,
The fallacy of our desires
And all the pride of life confute.

Farthest north. " Out of the north an evil shall break
forth upon all the inhabitants of the land."—Jeremiah, i. 14.
" For the king of the north shall return, and shall set forth
a multitude greater than the former, and shall certainly come
after certain years with a great army and with much riches."
— Daniel, xi. 13.

For they have watched since first
The world had birth,
And found sin in itself accursed,
And nothing permanent on earth.

SIR WILLIAM DAVENANT

(1606-1668)

I

SONG

The lark now leaves his wat'ry nest,
　And, climbing, shakes his dewy wings.
He takes this window for the east,
　And to implore your light, he sings:
Awake, awake, the morn will never rise ı
Till she can dress her beauty at your eyes.

I. *The lark now leaves his wat'ry nest.* An idea drawn
probably from *Venus and Adonis:*
　"Lo, here the gentle lark, weary of rest,
　　From her moist cabinet mounts up on high."
Then draw your curtains. A common conceit of the day.
Cf. Carew's *Celia Singing:*
　"You that think love can convey
　　　No other way
　　But through the eyes, into the heart
　　　His fatal dart,
　　Close up those casements."
DAVENANT. Godson of Shakespeare; perhaps his son.
"That notion of Sir William Davenant being more than a
poetical child only of Shakespeare was common in town; and
Sir William himself seemed fond of having it taken for
truth."— Spence's *Anecdotes.* Born, Oxford; educated, Lin-
coln College, 1620-1622; poet-laureate, 1638; governor of
King and Queen's Company of Players, 1639; refugee in
France during days of Cromwell; knighted, 1643; became
Roman Catholic; sent by the queen to Virginia, 1650, but
captured by Parliament; imprisoned in Tower, 1651-1653;
successful producer of plays; died, Lincoln's Inn Fields;

217

The merchant bows unto the seaman's star,
  The ploughman from the sun his season takes;
But still the lover wonders what they are
  Who look for day before his mistress wakes.
Awake, awake, break through your veils of lawn,
Then draw your curtains, and begin the dawn.

II

SONG

Why dost thou seem to boast, vainglorious sun?
  Why should thy bright complexion make thee proud?
Think but how often since thy race begun
  Thou wert eclipsed, then blush behind a cloud.

Or why look you, fair Empress of the night,
  So big upon't, when you at full appear?
Remember yours is but a borrowed light,
  Then shrink with paleness in your giddy sphere.

If neither sun nor moon can justify
  Their pride, how ill it women them befits,
That are on earth but *ignes fatui*
  That lead poor men to wander from their wits.

buried, Westminster Abbey. "There is not a more hopelessly
faded laurel on the slopes of the English Parnassus than
that which once flourished so bravely around the grotesque
head of Davenant."—Gosse, *Ward's English Poets*, Vol. II,
p. 289.

III

PRAISE AND PRAYER

Praise is devotion fit for mighty minds,
  The diff'ring world's agreeing sacrifice;
Where Heaven divided faiths united finds:
  But Prayer in various discord upward flies.

For Prayer the ocean is where diversely
  Men steer their course, each to a sev'ral coast;
Where all our interests so discordant be
  That half beg winds by which the rest are lost.

By Penitence when we ourselves forsake,
  'Tis but in wise design on piteous Heaven;
In Praise we nobly give what God may take,
  And are, without a beggar's blush, forgiven.

SIR JOHN SUCKLING

(1609-1642)

I

WHY SO PALE

Why so pale and wan, fond lover?
    Prithee, why so pale?
Will, when looking well can't move her,
    Looking ill prevail?
    Prithee, why so pale?

Why so dull and mute, young sinner?
    Prithee, why so mute?
Will, when speaking well can't win her,
    Saying nothing do 't?
    Prithee, why so mute?

Quit, quit, for shame! this will not move,
    This cannot take her;
If of herself she will not love,
    Nothing can make her:
    The devil take her!

SUCKLING. "For the next fifty years no one could write a
good love-song without more or less reminding the reader of
Suckling."— Gosse, *Ward's English Poets*, Vol. II, p. 171.
   I. WHY SO PALE? From Suckling's play, *Aglaura*, presented at Blackfriars in 1637. "'This is the very perfection
of the bantering, satirical lyric, in which the age of Charles
excelled."— Schelling, *Seventeenth Century Lyrics*, p. 251.

II

THE SIEGE

'T is now since I sat down before
  That foolish fort, a heart,
(Time strangely spent) a year or more,
  And still I did my part:

Made my approaches, from her hand
  Unto her lip did rise,
And did already understand
  The language of her eyes.

Proceeded on with no less art
  (My tongue was engineer),
I thought to undermine the heart
  By whispering in the ear.

When this did nothing, I brought down
  Great cannon-oaths, and shot
A thousand thousand to the town,
  And still it yielded not.

I then resolved to starve the place
  By cutting off all kisses,
Praying, and gazing on her face,
  And all such little blisses.

To draw her out, and from her strength,
  I drew all batteries in:
And brought myself to lie, at length,
  As if no siege had been.

When I had done what man could do,
  And thought the place mine own,
The enemy lay quiet, too,
  And smiled at all was done.

I sent to know from whence and where
  These hopes and this relief.
A spy informed, Honor was there,
  And did command in chief.

"March, march," quoth I, " the word straight give,
  Let's lose no time, but leave her;
That giant upon air will live,
  And hold it out for ever.

" To such a place our camp remove
  As will no siege abide;
I hate a fool that starves her love,
  Only to feed her pride."

III

CONSTANCY

Out upon it, I have loved
  Three whole days together;
And am like to love three more,
  If it prove fair weather.

Time shall moult away his wings,
  Ere he shall discover
In the whole wide world again
  Such a constant lover.

But the spite on 't is, no praise
  Is due at all to me;

III. *Out upon it.* " I admire Suckling's graceful audac-
ity. It is luckier to do a little thing surpassingly well than
a large thing indifferently so."— Locker-Lampson, *My Confidences*, p. 181.

Love with me had made no stays,
Had it any been but she.

Had it any been but she,
And that very face,
There had been at least ere this
A dozen dozen in her place.

IV

SONNET

Dost see how unregarded now
That piece of beauty passes?
There was a time when I did vow
To that alone;
But mark the fate of faces;
The red and white works now no more on me,
Than if it could not charm, or I not see.

And yet the face continues good,
And I have still desires,
And still the selfsame flesh and blood,
As apt to melt,
And suffer from those fires;
O, some kind power unriddle where it lies:
Whether my heart be faulty or her eyes?

She every day her man doth kill,
And I as often die;
Neither her power then or my will
Can questioned be.
What is the mystery?
Sure beauty's empire, like to greater states,
Have certain periods set, and hidden fates.

V

TRUE LOVE

No, no, fair heretic, it needs must be
 But an ill love in me,
  And worse for thee;
 For were it in my power
 To love thee now this hour
 More than I did the last,
  'T would then so fall,
 I might not love at all;
Love that can flow, and can admit increase,
Admits as well an ebb, and may grow less.

True love is still the same; the torrid zones
 And those more frigid ones
  It must not know:
 For love grown cold or hot
 Is lust or friendship, not
  The thing we have.
 For that's a flame would die,
 Held down or up too high:
Then think I love more than I can express,
And would love more, could I but love thee less.

V. TRUE LOVE. Prof. Schelling points out that this poem
shows the direct influence of Donne (*Seventeenth Century
Lyrics*, p. 251.) *Cf.* Donne's *Love's Growth.*

VI

SONG

I prithee send me back my heart,
　Since I cannot have thine;
For if from yours you will not part,
　Why then shouldst thou have mine?

Yet, now I think on 't, let it lie;
　To find it were in vain,
For th' hast a thief in either eye
　Would steal it back again.

Why should two hearts in one breast lie,
　And yet not lodge together?
O love, where is thy sympathy,
　If thus our breasts thou sever?

But love is such a mystery,
　I cannot find it out:
For when I think I'm best resolv'd,
　I then am most in doubt.

Then farewell care, and farewell woe!
　I will no longer pine;
For I'll believe I have her heart
　As much as she hath mine.

VI. Song. "Sir John Suckling . . . left far behind
him all former writers of song in gayety and ease." Hallam,
Introduction to the Literature of Europe, Pt. III, ch. v, par.
56.

VII

TRUTH IN LOVE

Of thee, kind boy, I ask no red and white,
 To make up my delight:
  No odd becoming graces,
Black eyes, or little know-not-whats in faces;
Make me but mad enough, give me good store
Of love for her I court:
  I ask no more,
'Tis love in love that makes the sport.

There's no such thing as that we beauty call,
 It is mere cosenage all;
  For though some long ago
Like certain colours mingled so and so,
That doth not tie me now from choosing new;
If I a fancy take
  To black and blue,
That fancy doth it beauty make.

'Tis not the meat, but 'tis the appetite
 Makes eating a delight,
  And if I like one dish
More than another, that a pheasant is;
What in our watches, that in us is found,—
So to the height and nick
  We up be wound,
No matter by what hand or trick.

VIII

A BALLAD UPON A WEDDING

I tell thee, Dick, where I have been,
Where I the rarest things have seen;
    O, things without compare!
Such sights again cannot be found
In any place on English ground,
    Be it at wake or fair.

At Charing-Cross, hard by the way,
Where we (thou know'st) do sell our hay,
    There is a house with stairs;
And there did I see coming down
Such folk as are not in our town,
    Forty, at least, in pairs.

Amongst the rest, one pest'lent fine
(His beard no bigger though than thine)
    Walked on before the rest:
Our landlord looks like nothing to him:
The King (God bless him) 'twould undo him,
    Should he go still so drest.

At Course-a-Park, without all doubt,
He should have first been taken out

VIII. A BALLAD UPON A WEDDING. "His famous ballad
of 'The Wedding' is the very perfection of gayety and arch-
ness in verse."— Craik. *A Compendious History of English
Literature*, Vol. II, p. 28.
    "Had he written nothing but 'A Ballad upon a Wedding,'
and the song beginning 'Why so pale and wan, fond lover?'
he would have earned his immortality. Their simplicity,
grace, and wit are unmatched and are peculiarly his own.
Their flavor is most rare; it delights at once and is never
forgotten."— Stokes, ed., *Poems of Suckling, preface.*

By all the maids i' th' town:
Though lusty Roger there had been,
Or little George upon the Green,
    Or Vincent of the Crown.

But wot you what? the youth was going
To make an end of all his wooing;
    The parson for him stay'd:
Yet by his leave (for all his haste)
He did not so much wish all past
    (Perchance), as did the maid.

The maid (and thereby hangs a tale),
For such a maid no Whitsun-ale
    Could ever yet produce:
No grape, that's kindly ripe, could be
So round, so plump, so soft as she,
    Nor half so full of juice.

Her finger was so small, the ring,
Would not stay on, which they did bring,
    It was too wide a peck:
And to say truth (for out it must)
It looked like the great collar (just)
    About our young colt's neck.

Her feet beneath her petticoat,
Like little mice, stole in and out,
    As if they fear'd the light:
But O she dances such a way!
No sun upon an Easter-day
    Is half so fine a sight.

Her cheeks so rare a white was on,
No daisy makes comparison,
    (Who sees them is undone),
For streaks of red were mingled there,
Such as are on a Catherine pear
    The side that's next the sun.

Her lips were red, and one was thin,
Compar'd to that was next her chin
    (Some bee had stung it newly);
But, Dick, her eyes so guard her face;
I durst no more upon them gaze
    Than on the sun in July.

Her mouth so small, when she does speak,
Thou'dst swear her teeth her words did break,
    That they might passage get;
But she so handled still the matter,
They came as good as ours, or better,
    And are not spent a whit.

Just in the nick the cook knocked thrice,
And all the waiters in a trice
    His summons did obey;
Each serving-man, with dish in hand,
Marched boldly up, like our trained band,
    Presented, and away.

When all the meat was on the table,
What man of knife or teeth was able
    To stay to be intreated?
And this the very reason was,
Before the parson could say grace,
    The company was seated.

The business of the kitchen's great,
For it is fit that men should eat;
    Nor was it there denied:
Passion o' me, how I run on!
There's that that would be thought upon
    (I trow) besides the bride.

Now hats fly off, and youths carouse;
Healths first go round, and then the house,
    The bride's came thick and thick:
And when 'twas nam'd another's health,
Perhaps he made it hers by stealth;
    And who could help it, Dick?

On the sudden up they rise and dance;
Then sit again and sigh, and glance:
    Then dance again and kiss:
Thus several ways the time did pass,
Whilst ev'ry woman wished her place,
    And every man wished his.

IX

THE LUTE SONG IN 'THE SAD ONE'

Hast thou seen the down in the air,
        When wanton blasts have tossed it?
Or the ship on the sea,
        When ruder winds have crossed it?
Hast thou marked the crocodile's weeping,
        Or the fox's sleeping?
Or hast viewed the peacock in his pride,
        Or the dove by his bride,
        When he courts for his lechery?
O so fickle, O so vain, O so false, so false is she!

IX. THE SAD ONE. One of Suckling's four decidedly poor plays.

WILLIAM CARTWRIGHT

(1611-1643)

I

A VALEDICTION

Bid me not go where neither suns nor showers
    Do make or cherish flowers;
Where discontented things in sadness lie
    And Nature grieves as I;
When I am parted from those eyes,
From which my better day doth rise,
    Though some propitious power
    Should plant me in a bower,
Where amongst happy lovers I might see
    How showers and sunbeams bring
    One everlasting spring,
Nor would those fall nor these shine forth to me:
    Nature to him is lost,
    Who loseth her he honors most.

CARTWRIGHT. "My son Cartwright wrote all like a man."
—Ben Jonson, *Preface, Cartwright's Poems.* Born, North-
way, near Tewkesbury; educated, Oxford; popular play
writer; after 1638 a clergyman; an officer in church of Salisbury, 1642; Junior Proctor of Oxford, 1643; at all times an
ardent admirer of Ben Jonson. "Cartwright . . . is to
us chiefly interesting as a type, . . . that of the typically
extravagant Oxford resident of his period."—A. W. Ward,
Ward's English Poets, Vol. II, p. 227.
    I. A VALEDICTION. "Few poems could better show the

Then fairest to my parting view display
 Your graces all in one full day,
Whose blessèd shapes I'll snatch and keep, till when
 I do return and view again:
So by this art fancy shall fortune cross,
And lovers live by thinking on their loss.

II

TO CUPID

Thou who didst never see the light,
Nor knowst the pleasure of the sight,
But always blinded, canst not say
Now it is night, or now 'tis day,
So captivate her sense, so blind her eye,
That still she love me, yet she ne'er know why.

Thou who dost wound us with such art,
We see no blood drop from the heart,
And, subtly cruel, leav'st no sign
To tell the blow or hand was thine,
O gently, gently wound my fair, that she
May thence believe the wound did come from me.

influence of Donne's subtle intellectual refinements than this
. . . Cartwright at his best, as here, seems to me to preserve also much of Donne's sincerity."— Schelling, *Seventeenth Century Lyrics*, p. 257.

RICHARD CRASHAW.

(1613-1649)

I

WISHES TO HIS SUPPOSED MISTRESS

Whoe'er she be,
That not impossible she,
That shall command my heart and me;

Where'er she lie,
Locked up from mortal eye,
In shady leaves of destiny:

Till that ripe birth
Of studied fate stand forth
And teach her fair steps tread our earth;

Till that divine
Idea take a shrine
Of crystal flesh, through which to shine:

Meet you her, my wishes,
Bespeak her to my blisses,
And be ye called, my absent kisses.

I. WISHES TO HIS SUPPOSED MISTRESS. It is easy to believe that the "mistress" is supposed, and not real. The
earthly love of man for woman was foreign to Crashaw's
nature.

I wish her beauty,
That owes not all its duty
To gaudy tire, or glist'ring shoe-tie.

Something more than
Taffeta or tissue can,
Or rampant feather, or rich fan.

More than the spoil
Of shop, or silkworm's toil,
Or a bought blush, or a set smile.

A face that's best
By its own beauty drest,
And can alone commend the rest.

A face made up
Out of no other shop
Than what Nature's white hand sets ope.

A cheek where youth
And blood, with pen of truth,
Write what the reader sweetly ru'th.

A cheek where grows
More than a morning rose:
Which to no box his being owes.

Lips where all day
A lover's kiss may play,
Yet carry nothing thence away.

Looks that oppress
Their richest tires, but dress
Themselves in simple nakedness.

Eyes that displace
The neighbor diamond, and out-face
That sunshine by their own sweet grace.

Tresses that wear
Jewels, but to declare
How much themselves more precious are,

Whose native ray
Can tame the wanton day
Of gems, that in their bright shades play.

Each ruby there,
Or pearl that dares appear,
Be its own blush, be its own tear.

A well-tamed heart,
For whose more noble smart
Love may be long choosing a dart.

Eyes that bestow
Full quivers on love's bow;
Yet pay less arrows than they owe.

Smiles that can warm
The blood, yet teach a charm,
That chastity shall take no harm.

Blushes that bin
The burnish of no sin,
Nor flames of aught too hot within.

Joys that confess
Virtue their mistress,
And have no other head to dress.

Fears, fond and flight
As the coy bride's when night
First does the longing lover right.

Tears, quickly fled,
And vain as those are shed
For a dying maidenhead.

Days that need borrow
No part of their good morrow
From a fore-spent night of sorrow.

Days that, in spite
Of darkness, by the light
Of a clear mind are day all night.

Nights, sweet as they,
Made short by lovers' play,
Yet long by th' absence of the day.

Life that dares send
A challenge to his end,
And when it comes, say, ' Welcome, friend.'

Sydneian showers
Of sweet discourse, whose powers
Can crown old Winter's head with flowers.

Soft silken hours,
Open suns, shady bowers,
'Bove all, nothing within that lowers.

Whate'er delight
Can make Day's forehead bright,
Or give down to the wings of Night.

In her whole frame
Have Nature all the name,
Art and ornament the shame.

Her flattery,
Picture and poesy:
Her counsel her own virtue be.

I wish her store
Of worth may leave her poor
Of wishes; and I wish — no more.

Now, if Time knows
That her, whose radiant brows
Weave them a garland of my vows;

Her whose just bays
My future hopes can raise,
A trophy to her present praise;

Her that dares be
What these lines wish to see:
I seek no further; it is she.

'Tis she, and here
Lo! I unclothe and clear
My wishes' cloudy character.

May she enjoy it,
Whose merit dare apply it,
But modesty dares still deny it.

Such worth as this is
Shall fix my flying wishes,
And determine them to kisses.

Let her full glory,
My fancies, fly before ye:
Be ye my fictions, but her story.

II

A SONG

Lord, when the sense of thy sweet grace
Sends up my soul to seek thy face,
Thy blessed eyes breed such desire
I die in love's delicious fire.
O Love, I am thy sacrifice,
Be still triumphant, blessed eyes;
Still shine on me, fair suns, that I
Still may behold though still I die.

Though still I die, I live again,
Still longing so to be still slain;
So painful is such loss of breath,
I die even in desire of death.
Still live in me this loving strife
Of living death and dying life:
For while thou sweetly slayest me,
Dead to myself, I live in thee.

III

ON THE ASSUMPTION OF THE VIRGIN MARY

Hark! she is called, the parting hour is come;
Take thy farewell, poor world. Heaven must go home.
A piece of heavenly earth; purer and brighter
Than the chaste stars, whose choice lamps come to light
        her,
Whilst through the crystal orbs, clearer than they,
She climbs, and makes a far more milky way.

She's called again; hark how the dear immortal dove
Sighs to his silver mate, " Rise up, my love,
Rise up, my fair, my spotless one,
The winter's past, the rain is gone;
The spring is come, the flowers appear,
No sweets, save thou, are wanting here.
Come away, my love,
Come away, my dove,
Cast off delay;
The court of heaven is come
To wait upon thee home;
Come away, come away!
The flowers appear,
Or quickly would, wert thou once here.
The spring is come, or if it stay
'Tis to keep time with thy delay.
The rain is gone, except so much as we
Detain in needful tears to weep the want of thee.
The winter's past,
Or if he make less haste,
His answer is, ' Why, she does so;
If summer come not, how can winter go? '
Come away, come away!
The shrill winds chide, the waters weep thy stay,
The fountains murmur, and each loftiest tree
Bows lowest his leafy top to look for thee.
Come away, my love,
Come away, my dove,
Cast off delay;

III. *Silver mate.* " Though ye have lain among the pots,
yet shall ye be as the wings of a dove covered with silver."—
Psalm lxviii. 13.
Rise up, my fair. " Rise up, my love, my fair one, and
come away. For, lo, the winter is past, the rain is over and
gone; the flowers appear on the earth; the time of the singing of birds is come and the voice of the turtle is heard in
our land; . . . O my dove, that art in the clefts of the
rock, in the secret place of the stairs, let me see thy countenance; let me hear thy voice; for sweet is thy voice, and thy
countenance is comely."—*Song of Solomon,* ii. 10-14.

The court of heaven is come
To wait upon thee home;
Come, come away."
She's called again. And will she go?
When heaven bids come, who can say no?
Heaven calls her, and she must away,
Heaven will not, and she cannot stay.
Go, then; go, glorious on the golden wings
Of the bright youth of heaven, that sings
Under so sweet a burden. Go,
Since thy dread son will have it so.
And while thou goest, our song and we
Will, as we may, reach after thee.
Hail, holy queen of humble hearts!
We in thy praise will have our parts.
And though thy dearest looks must now give light
To none but the blest heavens, whose bright
Beholders, lost in sweet delight,
Feed for ever their fair sight
With those divinest eyes, which we
And our dark world no more shall see;
Though our poor joys are parted so,
Yet shall our lips never let go
Thy gracious name, but to the last
Our loving song shall hold it fast.
Thy precious name shall be
Thyself to us, and we
With holy care will keep it by us.
We to the last
Will hold it fast,
And no assumption shall deny us.
All the sweetest showers
Of our fairest flowers
Will we strow upon it.
Though our sweets cannot make
It sweeter, they can take
Themselves new sweetness from it.

Maria, men and angels sing,
Maria, mother of our king.
Live, rosy princess, live, and may the bright
Crown of a most incomparable light
Embrace thy radiant brows! O may the best
Of everlasting joys bathe thy white breast.

Live, our chaste love, the holy mirth
Of heaven; the humble pride of earth.
Live, crown of women; queen of men;
Live, mistress of our song; and when
Our weak desires have done their best,
Sweet angels come, and sing the rest.

IV

THE FLAMING HEART

(Upon the book and picture of the Seraphical Saint
Theresa, as she is usually expressed with
a Seraphim beside her.)

.   .   .   .

O thou undaunted daughter of desires!
By all thy dower of lights and fires;
By all the eagle in thee, all the dove;
By all thy lives and deaths of love;
By thy large draughts of intellectual day,
And by thy thirsts of love more large than they;
By all thy brim-fill'd bowls of fierce desire,
By thy last morning's draught of liquid fire;

IV. THE FLAMING HEART. These lines follow a lengthy
and extremely artificial conceit which declares that a seraph's
arrow aimed at her heart would be consumed by flames, while
the heart would remain uninjured. "His masterpiece, one
of the most astonishing things in English or any other literature, comes without warning at the end of 'The Flaming
Heart.' . . . In a moment, in the twinkling of an eye,
without warning of any sort, the metre changes, the poet's
inspiration catches fire, and there rushes up into the heaven
of poetry this marvellous rocket of song."— Saintsbury, *History of Elizabethan Literature*, p. 384.

By the full kingdom of that final kiss
That seiz'd thy parting soul, and seal'd thee his;
By all the Heav'n thou hast in him
(Fair sister of the seraphim!)
By all of him we have in thee;
Leave nothing of myself in me.
Let me so read thy life, that I
Unto all life of mine may die.

RICHARD LOVELACE

(1618-1658)

I

SONG

Tell me not, sweet, I am unkind,
    That from the nunnery
Of thy chaste breast and quiet mind
    To war and arms I fly.

True, a new mistress now I chase,
    The first foe in the field;
And with a stronger faith embrace
    A sword, a horse, a shield.

Yet this inconstancy is such
    As you too shall adore:
I could not love thee, dear, so much
    Loved I not honor more.

II

TO ALTHEA FROM PRISON

When Love with unconfinèd wings,
    Hovers within my gates,
And my divine Althea brings
    To whisper at the grates;

I. Song. "'Going to the Wars,' his best poem, contains no line or part of a line that could by any possibility be improved."—Gosse, *Ward's English Poets*, Vol. II, p. 182.

II. To Althea. Set to music by Dr. John Wilson in *Cheerful Airs or Ballads*, 1660. "The first and fourth stanzas of this exquisite lyric would do honor to the most illustrious name."—Gosse, *Ward's English Poets*, Vol. II, p. 182. See the discussion of Lovelace for the cause of his imprisonment.

When I lie tangled in her hair
  And fettered to her eye,
The gods that wanton in the air
  Know no such liberty.

When flowing cups run swiftly round
  With no allaying Thames,
Our careless heads with roses crowned,
  Our hearts with loyal flames;
When thirsty grief in wine we steep,
  When healths and draughts go free,
Fishes that tipple in the deep
  Know no such liberty.

When, like committed linnets, I
  With shriller throat shall sing
The sweetness, mercy, majesty,
  And glories of my king;
When I shall voice aloud how good
  He is, how great should be,
Enlargèd winds, that curl the flood,
  Know no such liberty.

Stone walls do not a prison make,
  Nor iron bars a cage;
Minds innocent and quiet take
  That for a hermitage:
If I have freedom in my love,
  And in my soul am free,
Angels alone, that soar above,
  Enjoy such liberty.

When, like committed linnets, I. Changed by Bishop
Percy to "When linnet-like confined, I"; but Lovelace's
straightforward phrase is much better.

III

TO LUCASTA, GOING BEYOND THE SEAS

If to be absent were to be
Away from thee;
Or that when I am gone,
You or I were alone;
Then, my Lucasta, might I crave
Pity from blust'ring wind or swallowing wave.

But I'll not sigh one blast or gale
To swell my sail,
Or pay a tear to 'suage
The foaming blow-god's rage;
For whether he will let me pass
Or no, I'm still as happy as I was.

Though seas and land betwixt us both,
Our faith and troth,
Like separated souls,
All time and space controls:
Above the highest sphere we meet,
Unseen, unknown, and greet as angels greet.

So then we do anticipate
Our after fate,
And are alive i' th' skies,
If thus our lips and eyes
Can speak like spirits unconfined
In heaven, their earthly bodies left behind.

III. To LUCASTA. Set to music by Lawes in *Airs and Dialogues*, 1653-1658.
Blow-god. Probably Æolus, the god of winds.

IV

TO LUCASTA

Lucasta, frown, and let me die!
    But smile, and, see, I live!
The sad indifference of your eye
    Both kills and doth reprieve;
You hide our fate within its screen;
    We feel our judgment, e'er we hear;
So in one picture I have seen
    An angel here, the devil there!

V

THE SCRUTINY

Why shouldst thou swear I am forsworn,
    Since thine I vowed to be?
Lady, it is already morn,
    And 't was last night I swore to thee
    That fond impossibility.

Have I not loved thee much and long,
    A tedious twelve hours' space?
I should all other beauties wrong,
    And rob thee of a new embrace,
    Should I still dote upon thy face.

Not but all joy in thy brown hair
    By others may be found;
But I must search the black and fair,

V. THE SCRUTINY. *Cf.* Carew's *In the Person of a Lady* and Suckling's *Constancy.*

Like skilful min'ralists that sound
For treasure in un-plowed-up ground.

Then if, when I have loved my round,
  Thou prov'st the pleasant she,
With spoils of meaner beauties crowned,
  I laden will return to thee,
  E'en sated with variety.

VI

SONG

Amarantha, sweet and fair,
Ah, braid no more that shining hair;
As my curious hand or eye,
Hovering round thee, let it fly:
Let it fly as unconfined
As its ravisher, the wind,
Who has left his darling east
To wanton o'er this spicy nest.

Every tress must be confessed
But neatly tangled at the best,
Like a clew of golden thread,
Most excellently ravellèd,
Do not, then, wind up that light
In ribands, and o'ercloud the night,
Like the sun in's early ray,
But shake your head and scatter day.

VI. Song. In its compactness, neatness, pretty conceits,
and excellent development of one idea and *one only*, this song
is a good example of the better lyrics of the day.

ABRAHAM COWLEY

(1618-1667)

I

ANACRÈONTIQUE II
DRINKING

The thirsty earth soaks up the rain,
And drinks, and gapes for drink again.
The plants suck in the earth, and are
With constant drinking fresh and fair.
The sea itself, which one would think
Should have but little need of drink,
Drinks ten thousand rivers up,
So filled that they o'erflow the cup.
The busy sun — and one would guess
By's drunken fiery face no less—
Drinks up the sea, and when he has done,
The moon and stars drink up the sun;
They drink and dance by their own light,
They drink and revel all the night.
Nothing in Nature's sober found,
But an eternal health goes round.
Fill up the bowl, then, fill it high;
Fill all the glasses there, for why
Should every creature drink but I—
Why, men of morals, tell me why?

I. ANACREONTIQUE. "They [the Anacreontic Odes] are
smooth and elegant, and indeed the most agreeable and the
most perfect in their kind of all Mr. Cowley's poems."—
Blair, *Lectures on Rhetoric and Belles Lettres.*

II

THE CHRONICLE

Margarita first possessed,
If I remember well, my breast,
    Margarita first of all;
But when awhile the wanton maid
With my restless heart had played,
    Martha took the flying ball.

Martha soon did it resign
To the beauteous Catherine.
    Beauteous Catherine gave place
(Though loth and angry she to part
With the possession of my heart)
    To Elisa's conquering face.

Elisa till this hour might reign
Had she not evil counsels ta'en.
    Fundamental laws she broke,
And still new favorites she chose,
Till up in arms my passions rose,
    And cast away her yoke.

Mary, then, and gentle Ann
Both to reign at once began.
    Alternately they swayed;
And sometimes Mary was the fair,
And sometimes Ann the crown did wear;
    And sometimes both I obeyed.

II. THE CHRONICLE. "His praises are too far-sought and
too hyperbolical either to express love or to excite it; every
stage is crowded with darts and flames, with wounds and
death, with mangled souls and with broken hearts."— Johnson, *Lives of the English Poets: Cowley.* *Cf.* Herrick's *To
His Mistresses.*

Another Mary then arose
And did rigorous laws impose.
    A mighty tyrant she!
Long, alas, should I have been
Under that iron-sceptred queen,
    Had not Rebecca set me free.

When fair Rebecca set me free,
'Twas then a golden time with me;
    But soon those pleasures fled,
For the gracious princess died
In her youth and beauty's pride,
    And Judith reignèd in her stead.

One month, three days and half an hour
Judith held the sovereign power,
    Wondrous beautiful her face;
But so small and weak her wit,
That she to govern was unfit,
    And so Susanna took her place.

But when Isabella came,
Armed with a resistless flame
    And th' artillery of her eye,
Whilst she proudly marched about
Greater conquests to find out,
    She beat out Susan by the by.

But in her place I then obeyed
Black-eyed Bess, her viceroy-maid,
    To whom ensued a vacancy.
Thousand worse passions then possessed
The interregnum of my breast.
    Bless me from such an anarchy!

Gentle Henrietta then
And a third Mary next began,
    Then Joan, and Jane, and Audria.
And then a pretty Thomasine,
And then another Catherine,
    And then a long *et cœtera.*

But should I now to you relate
The strength and riches of their state,
    The powder, patches, and the pins,
The ribbands, jewels, and the rings,
The lace, the paint, and warlike things
    That make up all their magazines;

If I should tell the politic arts
To take and keep men's hearts,
    The letters, embassies and spies,
The frowns, and smiles, and flatteries,
The quarrels, tears and perjuries,
    Numberless, nameless mysteries!

And all the little lime-twigs laid
By Matchavil, the waiting-maid;
    I more voluminous should grow
(Chiefly if I like them should tell
All change of weathers that befell)
    Than Holinshed or Stow.

But I will briefer with them be,
Since few of them were long with me.
    An higher and a nobler strain
My present Emperess does claim,
Heleonora, first o' th' name;
    Whom God grant long to reign!

Matchavil. Macchiavelli, long looked upon as prince of schemers.

Holinshed or Stow. English chroniclers from whom dramatists, especially Shakespeare, have drawn much material.

III

THE INCONSTANT

I never yet could see that face
    Which had no dart for me;
From fifteen years, to fifty's space,
    They all victorious be.
Love, thou'rt a devil, if I may call thee *one;*
For sure in me thy name is Legion.

Color or shape, good limbs or face,
    Goodness or wit, in all I find,
In motion or in speech, a grace;
    If all fail, yet 'tis womankind;
And I'm so weak, the pistol need not be
Double or treble charged to murder me.

If tall, the name of 'proper' slays;
    If fair, she's pleasant in the light;
If low, her prettiness does please;
    If black, what lover loves not night?
If yellow-haired, I love lest it should be
Th' excuse to others for not loving me.

The fat, like plenty, fills my heart;
    The lean, with love makes me too so;
If straight, her body's Cupid's dart
    To me; if crooked, 'tis his bow:
Nay, age itself does me to rage incline,
And strength to women gives, as well as wine.

III. *Proper.* Pretty.
If black. The adjective *black* was frequently used by
poets of the day to intimate a suspicion of evil or immorality.

Just half as large as Charity
    My richly landed Love's become;
And, judged aright, is Constancy,
    Though it take up a larger room:
Him who loves always one, why should they call
More constant than the man loves always all?

Thus with unwearied wings I flee
    Through all Love's gardens and his fields;
And, like the wise, industrious bee,
    No weed but honey to me yields!
Honey still spent this dil'gence still supplies,
Though I return not home with laden thighs.

My soul at first indeed did prove
    Of pretty strength against a dart,
Till I this habit got of love;
    But my consumed and wasted heart,
Once burnt to tinder with a strong desire,
Since that, by every spark is set on fire.

IV

THE SPRING

Though you be absent here, I needs must say
The trees as beauteous are, and flowers as gay,
    As ever they were wont to be;
    Nay, the birds' rural music, too,
    Is as melodious and free
    As if they sung to pleasure you:
I saw a rose-bud ope this morn; I'll swear
The blushing morning open'd not more fair.

How could it be so fair, and you away?
How could the trees be beauteous, flowers so gay?
　　Could they remember but last year,
　　How you did them, they you delight,
　　The sprouting leaves which saw you here,
　　And call'd their fellows to the sight,
Would, looking round for the same sight in vain,
Creep back into their silent barks again.

Where'er you walked trees were as reverend made
As when of old gods dwelt in every shade.
　　Is't possible they should not know
　　What loss of honour they sustain,
　　That thus they smile and flourish now,
　　And still their former pride retain?
Dull creatures! 'tis not without cause that she,
Who fled the god of wit, was made a tree.

In ancient times sure they much wiser were,
When they rejoic'd the Thracian verse to hear;
　　In vain did Nature bid them stay,
　　When Orpheus had his song begun;
　　They call'd their wondering roots away,
　　And bade them silent to him run.
How would those learned trees have followed you?
You would have drawn them, and their poet, too.

But who can blame them now? for, since you're gone,
They're here the only fair, and shine alone.
　　You did their natural rights invade;
　　Where ever you did walk or sit,
　　The thickest boughs could make no shade,
　　Although the sun had granted it:
The fairest flowers could please no more, near you,
Than painted flowers, set next to them, could do.

When e'er then you come hither, that shall be
The time, which this to others is, to me.
   The little joys which here are now,
   The name of punishments do bear,
   When by their sight they let us know
   How we depriv'd of greater are.
'Tis you the best of seasons with you bring;
This is for beasts, and that for men the spring.

V

A VOTE

This only grant me, that my means may lie
Too low for envy, for contempt too high.
   Some honor I would have,
Not from great deeds, but good alone:
Th' unknown are better than ill-known;
   Rumor can ope the grave.
Acquaintance I would have, but when't depends
Not on the number, but the choice of friends.

Books should, not business, entertain the light;
And sleep, as undisturbed as death, the night.
   My house a cottage, more
Than palace, and should fitting be
For all my use, no luxury.
   My garden painted o'er
With Nature's hand, not Art's; and pleasures yield
Horace might envy in his Sabine field.

V. A VOTE. The word here means a keen desire or longing. The stanzas given are only the last three — those se-
lected by Cowley for a volume in 1661. As pointed out by
the author himself, he was influenced by Horace in the writing of this poem.

Thus would I double my life's fading space,
For he that runs it well, twice runs his race.
  And in this true delight,
These unbought sports, this happy state,
I would not fear nor wish my fate,
  But boldly say each night:
To-morrow let my sun his beams display,
Or in clouds hide them: I have lived to-day.

VI

THE WISH

Well, then, I now do plainly see
This busy world and I shall ne'er agree;
The very honey of all earthly joy
  Does of all meats the soonest cloy,
  And they, methinks, deserve my pity
Who for it can endure the stings,
The crowd, and buzz, and murmurings
  Of this great hive, the city.

Ah, yet, ere I descend to th' grave
May I a small house and a large garden have!
And a few friends, and many books, both true,
  Both wise, and both delightful, too!
  And since love ne'er will from me flee,
A mistress moderately fair,
And good as guardian-angels are,
  Only belov'd, and loving me!

O fountains, when in you shall I
Myself, eased of unpeaceful thoughts, espy?
O fields! O woods! when, when shall I be made
  The happy tenant of your shade?

Here's the spring-head of pleasure's flood;
Where all the riches lie, that she
        Has coin'd and stamp'd for good.

Pride and ambition here,
Only in far-fetched metaphors appear;
Here nought but winds can hurtful murmurs scatter,
        And nought but echo flatter.
The gods, when they descended, hither
From heav'n did always choose their way;
And therefore we may boldly say,
        That 'tis the way too thither.

How happy here should I
And one dear she live, and embracing lie!
She who is all the world, and can exclude
        In deserts solitude.
I should have then this only fear,
Lest men, when they my pleasures see,
Should hither throng to live like me,
        And make a city here.

VI. *And make a city here.* In spite of the far-stretched
nature of such conceits, we can but admire the ingenuity
that was evidenced in their making.

SIR EDWARD SHERBURNE

(1618-1702)

I

WEEPING AND KISSING

A kiss I begged, but smiling she
    Denied it me;
When straight, her cheeks with tears o'erflown—
    Now kinder grown—
What smiling she'd not let one have
    She weeping gave.
Then you whom scornful beauties awe,
    Hope yet relief
From Love, who tears from smiles can draw,
    Pleasure from grief.

SHERBURNE. Born, St. Giles' Cripplegate, London; clerk
of the ordinance, 1641; ejected by the House of Lords for
adhering to the king; joined Charles' army and retired with
him to Oxford, where he was made Master of Arts; restored
to clerkship at the Restoration; knighted by Charles II;
ejected from office on abdication of James II; suffered
much for the royal cause and at one time lost his all, in-
cluding a rare library. His verses are frequently found in
Wit's Recreations.

II

THE VOW.

By my life I vow
That my life art thou,
By my heart and by my eyes;
But thy faith denies
To my juster oath t' incline,
For thou say'st I swear by thine.

By this sigh I swear,
By this falling tear,
By the undeservèd pains
My griev'd soul sustains:
Now thou may'st believe my moan,
These are too, too much my own.

ANDREW MARVELL

(1621-1678)

I

THE FAIR SINGER

To make a final conquest of all me,
Love did compose so sweet an enemy,
In whom both beauties to my death agree,
Joining themselves in fatal harmony;
That, while she with her eyes my heart does bind,
She with her voice might captivate my mind.

I could have fled from one but singly fair;
My disentangled soul itself might save,
Breaking the curlèd trammels of her hair;
But how should I avoid to be her slave
Whose subtle art invisibly can wreathe
My fetters of the very air I breathe?

MARVELL. "A man endowed by Nature, so improved by
Education, Study, and Travel, so consummated by Experience, that joining the peculiar graces of Wit and Learning
with a singular penetration and strength of judgment; and
exercising all these in the whole course of his life, with an
unalterable steadiness in the ways of Virtue, he became
the ornament and example of his age, beloved by good men,
feared by bad, admired by all, though imitated by few; and
scarce paralleled by any." — *Inscription on Marvell's Monument, 1688.* Born, Winstead-in-Holderness, Yorks.; educated, Hull Grammar School and Trinity College, Cambridge; secretary and amanuensis to Milton; recommended
by Milton as assistant Latin secretary, 1652; afterwards
joint secretary with Milton; member of Parliament, 1660-
1661; conspicuous for his brave condemnation of the loose
life of Charles II; died, London.

It had been easy fighting in some plain,
Where victory might hang in equal choice;
But all resistance against her is vain
Who has th' advantage both of eyes and voice;
And all my forces needs must be undone,
She having gainèd both the wind and sun.

II

THE MOWER'S SONG

My mind was once the true survey
Of all these meadows fresh and gay,
And in the greenness of the grass
Did see its hopes as in a glass;
When Juliana came, and she,
What I do to the grass, does to my thoughts and me.

But these, while I with sorrow pine,
Grew more luxuriant still and fine,
That not one blade of grass you spied
But had a flower on either side;
When Juliana came, and she,
What I do to the grass, does to my thoughts and me.

Unthankful meadows, could you so
A fellowship so true forego,
And in your gaudy May-games meet,
While I lay trodden under feet—
When Juliana came, and she,
What I do to the grass, does to my thoughts and me?

But what you in compassion ought,
Shall now by my revenge be wrought;
And flowers, and grass, and I, and all,
Will in one common ruin fall;

II. *True survey.* Copy or map.

For Juliana comes, and she,
What I do to the grass, does to my thoughts and me.

And thus, ye meadows, which have been
Companions of my thoughts more green,
Shall now the heraldry become
With which I shall adorn my tomb;
For Juliana came, and she,
What I do to the grass, does to my thoughts and me.

III

TO HIS COY MISTRESS

Had we but world enough and time,
This coyness, lady, were no crime.
We would sit down and think which way
To walk and pass our long love's day.
Thou by the Indian Ganges' side
Shouldst rubies. find; I by the tide
Of Humber would complain.   I would
Love you ten years before the Flood;
And you should, if you please, refuse
Till the conversion of the Jews.
My vegetable love should grow
Vaster than empires, and more slow;
An hundred years should go to praise
Thine eyes and on thy forehead gaze;
Two hundred to adore each breast,

III. To His Coy Mistress. At no time did Marvell carry
into practice the theories here set forth. "In a Court which
held no man to be honest and no woman chaste, . . .
Marvell, revering and respecting himself, was proof against
its charms."— H. Coleridge, *Biographia Borealis*, p. 57.

But thirty thousand to the rest;
An age at least to every part;
And the last age should show your heart.
For, lady, you deserve this state,
Nor would I love at lower rate.

But at my back I always hear
Time's wingèd chariot hurrying near;
And yonder all before us lie
Deserts of vast eternity.
Thy beauty shall no more be found,
Nor, in thy marble vault, shall sound
My echoing song; then worms shall try
That long preserved virginity;
And your quaint honor turn to dust,
And into ashes all my lust:
The grave's a fine and private place,
But none, I think, do there embrace.

Now, therefore, while the youthful hue
Sits on thy skin like morning dew,
And while thy willing soul transpires
At every pore with instant fires,
Now let us sport us while we may,
And now, like amorous birds of prey,
Rather at once our time devour
Than languish in his slow-chapt power.
Let us roll all our strength, and all
Our sweetness up into one ball;
And tear our pleasures with rough strife
Thorough the iron gates of life:
Thus, though we cannot make our sun
Stand still, yet we will make him run.

Your quaint honor. Quaint means here old-fashioned, out-
of-date, curious.

IV

THE GARDEN

How vainly men themselves amaze,
To win the palm, the oak, or bays,
And their incessant labors see
Crowned from some single herb, or tree,
Whose short and narrow-verged shade
Does prudently their toils upbraid,
While all the flowers and trees do close
To weave the garlands of repose!

Fair Quiet, have I found thee here,
And Innocence, thy sister dear?
Mistaken long, I sought you then
In busy companies of men.
Your sacred plants, if here below,
Only among the plants will grow;
Society is all but rude
To this delicious solitude.

No white nor red was ever seen
So amorous as this lovely green.
Fond lovers, cruel as their flame,
Cut in these trees their mistress' name.
Little, alas! they know or heed
How far these beauties her exceed!
Fair trees! where'er your barks I wound,
No name shall but your own be found.

IV. The Garden. "In it . . . he shows a depth of poetic feeling wonderful in a political gladiator."— Goldwin Smith, *Ward's English Poets*, Vol. II, p. 384.

When we have run our passion's heat,
Love hither makes his best retreat.
The gods, who mortal beauty chase,
Still in a tree did end their race;
Apollo hunted Daphne so,
Only that she might a laurel grow;
And Pan did after Syrinx speed,
Not as a nymph, but for a reed.

What wondrous life is this I lead!
Ripe apples drop about my head;
The luscious clusters of a vine
Upon my mouth do crush their wine;
The nectarine, and curious peach,
Into my hands themselves do reach;
Stumbling on melons, as I pass,
Ensnared with flowers, I fall on grass.

Meanwhile the mind, from pleasure less,
Withdraws into its happiness;—
The mind, that ocean where each kind
Does straight its own resemblance find;
Yet it creates, transcending these,
Far other worlds, and other seas,
Annihilating all that's made
To a green thought in a green shade.

Here at the fountain's sliding foot,
Or at some fruit-tree's mossy root,
Casting the body's vest aside,
My soul into the boughs does glide:
There, like a bird, it sits and sings,
Then whets and claps its silver wings,
And, till prepared for longer flight,
Waves in its plumes the various light.

Such was that happy garden-state,
While man there walked without a mate:
After a place so pure and sweet,
What other help could yet be meet!
But 'twas beyond a mortal's share
To wander solitary there:
Two paradises are in one,
To live in paradise alone.

How well the skilful gardener drew
Of flowers, and herbs, this dial new,
Where, from above, the milder sun
Does though a fragrant zodiac run,
And, as it works, the industrious bee
Computes its time as well as we!
How could such sweet and wholesome hours
Be reckoned but with herbs and flowers?

HENRY VAUGHAN

(1622-1695)

I

TO AMORET, GONE FROM HOME

Fancy and I last evening walked,
And, Amoret, of thee we talked.
The west just then had stol'n the sun,
And his last blushes were begun.
We sate, and marked how everything
Did mourn his absence; how the spring
That smiled and curled about his beams,
Whilst he was here, now checked her streams;
The wanton eddies of her face
Were taught less noise and smoother grace;
And in a slow, sad channel went,
Whisp'ring the banks their discontent.
The careless banks of flowers that spread
Their perfumed bosoms to his head,
And, with an open, free embrace,
Did entertain his beamy face,
Like absent friends point to the west,
And on that weak reflection feast.

VAUGHAN. Known as the Silurist because of his residence
in a portion of Wales called *Siluria* by the Roman invaders.
Born, Llansaintfread, Brecknockshire, Wales; educated, Oxford; studied medicine, London; spent most of his life within
his Welsh parish; at all times an ardent Royalist.

If creatures, then, that have no sense,
But the loose tie of influence—
　　Though fate and time each day remove
　　Those things that element their love—
At such vast distance can agree,
Why, Amoret, why should not we?

II

THE WORLD

I saw Eternity the other night
Like a great ring of pure and endless light,
　　All calm, as it was bright;
And round beneath it Time, in hours, days, years,
　　Driv'n by the spheres,
Like a vast shadow moved, in which the world
　　And all her train were hurled.
The doating lover in his quaintest strain
　　Did there complain;
Near him, his lute, his fancy, and his flights,
　　Wit's four delights,
With gloves and knots, the silly snares of pleasure;
　　Yet his dear treasure
All scattered lay, while he his eyes did pour
　　Upon a flower.

II. THE WORLD. In the original this poem is followed
by the words of I John. ii, 16, 17: "For all that is in the
world, the lust of the flesh, and the lust of the eyes, and the
pride of life, is not of the Father, but is of the world, and
the world passeth away, and the lust thereof; but he that
doeth the will of God abideth forever."
I saw Eternity. "Eternity has been known to spoil a
poet for time, but not in this instance."— Quincey, *A Little
English Gallery,* p. 59.

The darksome statesman, hung with weights and woe,
Like a thick midnight-fog, moved there so slow
    He did not stay nor go;
Condemning thoughts, like sad eclipses, scowl
    Upon his soul,
And clouds of crying witnesses without
    Pursued him with one shout;
Yet digged the mole, and, lest his ways be found,
    Worked under ground,
Where he did clutch his prey.   But one did see
    That policy:
Churches and altars fed him; perjuries
    Were gnats and flies;
It rained about him blood and tears; but he
    Drank them as free.

The fearful miser on a heap of rust
Sate pining all his life there, did scarce trust
    His own hands with the dust;
Yet would not place one piece above, but lives
    In fear of thieves.
Thousands were as frantic as himself
    And hugged each one his pelf;
The downright epicure placed heaven in sense,
    And scorned pretence;
While others, slipped into a wide excess,
    Said little less;
The weaker sort slight, trivial wares enslave,
    Who think them brave;
And poor despisèd Truth sate counting by
    Their victory.

Yet some, who all this time did weep and sing,
And sing and weep, soared up into the ring;
    But most would use no wing:
" O fools," said I, " thus to prefer dark night

The fearful miser. Full of fear, alarmed.
Place one piece above. In heaven.

Before true light!
To live in grots and caves, and hate the day
    Because it shows the way,
The way, which from this dead and dark abode
    Leads up to God;
A way where you might tread the sun, and be
    As bright as he!"
But, as I did their madness so discuss,
    One whispered thus:
" This ring the bridegroom did for none provide
    But for his bride."

III

PEACE

My soul, there is a country
    Afar beyond the stars,
Where stands a wingèd sentry
    All skilful in the wars,
There, above noise and danger,
    Sweet Peace sits crowned with smiles,
And one born in a manger
    Commands the beauteous files.
He is thy gracious friend
    And — O my soul, awake!—
Did in pure love descend
    To die here for thy sake.
If thou canst get but thither,
    There grows the flower of peace,
The rose that cannot wither,
    Thy fortress and thy ease.
Leave then thy foolish ranges;
    For none can thee secure,
But one, who never changes,
    Thy God, thy life, thy cure.

III. *Thy foolish ranges.* Aimless wanderings.

IV.

BEYOND THE VEIL

They are all gone into the world of light!
    And I alone sit lingering here;
Their very memory is fair and bright,
    And my sad thoughts doth clear.

It glows and glitters in my cloudy breast,
    Like stars upon some gloomy grove,
Or those faint beams in which this hill is drest,
    After the sun's remove.

I see them walking in an air of glory,
    Whose light doth trample on my days:
My days, which are at best but dull and hoary,
    Mere glimmering and decays.

O holy Hope! and high Humility,
    High as the heavens above!
These are your walks, and you have showed them me,
    To kindle my cold love.

Dear, beauteous Death! the jewel of the just,
    Shining nowhere but in the dark,
What mysteries do lie beyond thy dust,
    Could man outlook that mark!

He that hath found some fledged bird's nest may know
    At first sight if the bird be flown;
But what fair well or grove he sings in now,
    That is to him unknown.

IV. *He that hath found.* A stanza worthy of a far
greater poet. Its thought and its Anglo-Saxon directness
combine to make it near perfection.

And yet as angels in some brighter dreams
  Call to the soul, when man doth sleep,
So some strange thoughts transcend our wonted themes,
  And into glory peep.

If a star were confined into a tomb,
  The captive flames must needs burn there;
But when the hand that locked her up gives room,
  She'll shine through all the sphere.

O Father of eternal life, and all
  Created glories under thee,
Resume thy spirit from this world of thrall
  Into true liberty.

Either disperse these mists, which blot and fill
  My perspective still as they pass,
Or else remove me hence unto that hill
  Where I shall need no glass.

And yet as angels. This stanza seems somewhat a fore-
runner of Wordsworth's *Intimations of Immortality.*

If a star were confined. A splendid thought. Here the
soul is hampered by the flesh; but in the hereafter it shall
shine in all its intrinsic glory.

THOMAS STANLEY

(1625-1678)

I

THE RELAPSE

O turn away those cruel eyes,
   The stars of my undoing;
Or death in such a bright disguise
   May tempt a second wooing.

Punish their blind and impious pride
   Who dare condemn thy glory;
It was my fall that deified
   Thy name and sealed thy story.

Yet no new suffering can prepare
   A higher praise to crown thee;
Though my first death proclaim thee fair,
   My second will unthrone thee.

Lovers will doubt thou can'st entice
   No other for thy fuel,
And if thou burn one victim twice,
   Both think thee poor and cruel.

STANLEY. "In him the series of writers called 'Metaphysical' closes."— Gosse, *Ward's English Poets,* Vol. II, p. 286. Born, Cumberlow — Green, Hertfordshire; educated, Cambridge; student, Middle Temple; published first volume of his once famous *History of Philosophy,* 1655, soon followed by three other volumes; died, London. Practically all of his poetry was written in his college days.

II

CELIA SINGING

Roses in breathing forth their scent,
Or stars their borrowed ornament,
Nymphs in watery sphere that move,
Or angels in their orbs above,
The wingèd chariot of the light,
Or the slow, silent wheels of night,
The shade which from the swifter sun
Doth in a circular motion run,
Or souls that their eternal rest do keep,
Make far more noise than Celia's breath in sleep.

But if the angel, which inspires
This subtle flame with active fires,
Should mould his breath to words, and those
Into a harmony dispose,
The music of this heavenly sphere
Would steal each soul out at the ear,
And into plants. and stones infuse
A life that cherubim would choose,
And with new powers invert the laws of fate,
Kill those that live, and dead things animate.

III

THE TOMB

When, cruel fair one, I am slain
By thy disdain,
And, as a trophy of thy scorn,
To some old tomb am borne,

Thy fetters must their power bequeath
 To those of Death;
Nor can thy flame immortal burn,
Like monumental fires within an urn;
Thus, freed from thy proud empire, I shall prove
There is more liberty in Death than Love.

And when forsaken lovers come
 To see my tomb,
Take heed thou mix not with the crowd
 And, as a victor, proud
To view the spoils thy beauty made,
 Press near my shade,
Lest thy too cruel breath or name
Should fan my ashes back into a flame,
 And thou, devoured by this revengeful fire,
His sacrifice, who died as thine, expire.

But if cold earth or marble must
 Conceal my dust,
Whilst hid in some dark ruins, I
 Dumb and forgotten lie,
The pride of all thy victory
 Will sleep with me;
And they who should attest thy glory,
Will, or forget, or not believe this story,
Then, to increase thy triumph, let me rest,
Since by thine eye slain, buried in thy breast.

CHARLES COTTON

(1630-1687)

I

ODE

Fair Isabel, if aught but thee
  I could, or would, or like, or love;
  If other beauties but approve
To sweeten my captivity:
  I might those passions be above,
    Those powerful passions, that combine
    To make and keep me only thine.

Or if for tempting treasure, I
  Of the world's god, prevailing gold,
  Could see thy love and my truth sold,
A greater, nobler treasury:
  My flame to thee might then grow cold,
    And I, like one whose love is sense,
    Exchange thee for convenience.

COTTON. "The noblest of our youth and best of friends."—
Lovelace, *Dedication, The Triumph of Philamore and Amoret,*
1649. Born, Beresford, Staffordshire; once well known as a
translator of Montaigne's *Essays;* a close friend of Izaak
Walton and an enthusiastic angler; wrote as a second part
to Walton's *Complete Angler* a treatise on fishing with the
fly; a lover of books and country life; died, Westminster.
    I. *Fair Isabel.* Probably Isabella Hutchinson, whom he
married in 1656.

But when I vow to thee I do
  Love thee above or health or peace,
  Gold, joy, and all such toys as these,
'Bove happiness and honor, too:
    Thou then must know this love can cease
    Nor change, for all the glorious show
    Wealth and discretion bribes us to.

What such a love deserves, thou, sweet,
  As knowing best, mayst best reward;
  I, for thy bounty well prepared,
With open arms my blessing meet.
    Then do not, dear, our joys retard;
    But unto him propitious be
    That knows no love, nor life, but thee.

II

SONG

Join once again, my Celia, join
Thy rosy lips to these of mine,
  Which, though they be not such,
Are full as sensible of bliss,
That is, as soon can taste a kiss,
  As thine of softer touch.

Each kiss of thine creates desire,
Thy odorous breath inflames love's fire,
  And wakes the sleeping coal:
Such a kiss to be I find
The conversation of the mind,
  And whisper of the soul.

Thanks, sweetest, now thou'rt perfect grown,
For by this last kiss I'm undone;
  Thou breathest silent darts,
Henceforth each little touch will prove
A dangerous stratagem in love,
  And thou wilt blow up hearts.

III

LAURA SLEEPING

Winds, whisper gently whilst she sleeps,
  And fan her with your cooling wings,
Whilst she her drops of beauty weeps
  From pure and yet unrivalled springs.

Glide over beauty's field, her face,
  To kiss her lip and cheek be bold,
But with a calm and stealing pace,
  Neither too rude nor yet too cold.

Play in her beams and crisp her hair
  With such a gale as wings soft love,
And with so sweet, so rich an air
  As breathes from the Arabian grove.

A breath as hushed as lover's sigh,
  Or that unfolds the morning door;
Sweet as the winds that gently fly
  To sweep the spring's enamelled floor.

Murmur soft music to her dreams,
  That pure and unpolluted run,
Like to the new-born crystal streams
  Under the bright enamoured sun.

But when she waking shall display
  Her light, retire within your bar.
Her breath is life, her eyes are day,
  And all mankind her creatures are.

IV

RONDEAU

Forbear, fair Phyllis, O forbear
Those deadly killing frowns, and spare
A heart so loving and so true,
By none to be subdued but you,
Who my poor life's sole princess are.
You only can create my care;
But offend you, I all things dare.
Then, lest your cruelty you rue,
            Forbear;
And lest you kill that heart, beware,
To which there is some pity due,
If but because I humbly sue.
Your anger, therefore, sweetest fair,
Though mercy in your sex is rare,
            Forbear.

RONDEAU. A French form of verse brought into some popularity in the days of Wyatt (1503-1542), but used by scarcely any English poet, save Cotton, until its sudden popularity in the nineteenth century.

CHARLES SACKVILLE

(1637-1706)

I

SONG

Phyllis, for shame! let us improve
   A thousand different ways
Those few short moments snatched by love
   From many tedious days.

If you want courage to despise
   The censure of the grave,
Though Love's a tyrant in your eyes,
   Your heart is but a slave.

My love is full of noble pride,
   Nor can it e'er submit
To let that fop, Discretion, ride
   In triumph over it.

SACKVILLE. Earl of Dorset. "He was the finest gentleman of the voluptuous Court of Charles II and in the gloomy
one of King William."—Walpole, *Noble Authors*, II, p. 96.
Earl of Middlesex, 1675; Earl of Dorset, 1677; distinguished
himself in House of Commons; served in the first Dutch War,
1665; opposed James II and aided the cause of William; no-
torious for his indecent wildness; died, Bath. He wrote many
satirical poems, but is remembered by his song, "To all you
ladies now at land." "He was a man whose elegance and
judgment were universally confessed, and whose bounty to
the learned and witty was generally known."—Johnson,
Lives of the English Poets.

False friends I have, as well as you,
   Who daily counsel me
Fame and ambition to pursue,
   And leave off loving thee.

But when the least regard I show
   To fools who thus advise,
May I be dull enough to grow
   Most miserably wise!

II

ON A LADY

Dorinda's sparkling wit and eyes
   United cast too fierce a light,
Which blazes high, but quickly dies,
   Pains not the heart, but hurts the sight.

Love is a calmer, gentler joy;
   Smooth are his looks, and soft his pace:
Her Cupid is a blackguard boy
   That runs his link full in your face.

III

SONG

To all you ladies now at land
   We men at sea indite;
But first would have you understand
   How hard it is to write:

II. ON A LADY. Probably Catherine Sedley, Countess of Dorchester.
   Blackguard boy. A link boy, a boy employed to carry a torch to guide parties through the streets.
   III. SONG. "'To all you ladies' is an admitted masterpiece."— Garnett, *Dictionary of National Biography,* Vol. I, p. 87.

The Muses now, and Neptune, too,
. We must implore to write to you—
,With a fa, la, la, la, la!

For though the Muses should prove kind,
    And fill our empty brain,
,Yet if rough Neptune rouse the wind
    To wave the azure main,
Our paper, pen, and ink, and we,
Roll up and down our ships at sea—
    ,With a fa, la, la, la, la!

Then, if we write not by each post,
    Think not we are unkind;
Nor yet conclude our ships are lost
    By Dutchmen or by wind:
Our tears we'll send a speedier way,
The tide shall bring them twice a day—
    ,With a fa, la, la, la, la!

The King with wonder and surprise
    Will swear the seas grow bold,
Because the tides will higher rise
    Than e'er they did of old;
But let him know it is our tears
Bring floods of grief to Whitehall stairs—
    ,With a fa, la, la, la, la!

Should foggy 'Opdam chance to know
    Our sad and dismal story,
,The Dutch would scorn so weak a foe,
    And quit their fort at Goree;
For what resistance can they find
From men who've left their hearts behind?—
    With a fa, la, la, la, la!

Let wind and weather do its worst,
  Be you to us but kind;
Let Dutchmen vapour, Spaniards curse,
  No sorrow we shall find;
'Tis then, no matter how things go,
Or who's our friend or who's our foe—
    With a fa, la, la, la, la!

To pass our tedious hours away
  We throw a merry main,
Or else at serious ombre play;
  But why should we in vain
Each other's ruin thus pursue?
We were undone when we left you—
    With a fa, la, la, la, la!

But now our fears tempestuous grow
  And cast our hopes away,
Whilst you, regardless of our woe,
  Sit careless at a play,
Perhaps permit some happier man
To kiss your hand or flirt your fan—
    With a fa, la, la, la, la!

When any mournful tune you hear
  That dies in every note,
As if it sigh'd with each man's care
  For being so remote,
Think then how often love we've made
To you, when all those tunes were play'd—
    With a fa, la, la, la, la!

In justice you cannot refuse
  To think of our distress,
When we for hopes of honour lose
  Our certain happiness:

All those designs are but to prove
Ourselves more worthy of your love—
  With a fa, la, la, la, la!

And now we've told you all our loves,
  And likewise all our fears,
In hopes this declaration moves
  Some pity for our tears:
Let's hear of no inconstancy—
We have too much of that at sea—
  With a fa, la, la, la, la!

SIR CHARLES SEDLEY

(1639?-1701)

I

TO CELIA

Not, Celia, that I juster am,
　　Or better than the rest;
For I would change each hour like them
　　Were not my heart at rest.

But I am tied to very thee
　　By every thought I have;
Thy face I only care to see,
　　Thy heart I only crave.

All that in woman is adored
　　In thy dear self I find;
For the whole sex can but afford
　　The handsome and the kind.

SEDLEY. Born, Aylesford, Kent; educated, Wadham College, Oxford; succeeded to baronetcy, 1656; member of parliament, 1668-1681, 1690-1695, and 1696-1701; a vigorous pamphleteer and satirist; opposed to the Stuarts in the Revolution. In his earlier days he led a wildly dissipated life. " Pierce do tell me, among other news, the late frolick and debauchery of Sir Charles Sedley and Buckhurst, running up and down all the night, almost naked, through the streets; and at last fighting and being beat by the watch and clapped all night, and how the king takes their parts; and my Lord Chief Justice Keeling hath laid the constable by the heels to answer it next Session, which is a horrid shame."— Pepys, *Diary, Oct. 23, 1668.*

Why, then, should I seek further store
  And still make love anew?
When change itself can give no more,
  'Tis easy to be true.

II

SONG

Love still has something of the sea,
  From whence his mother rose;
No time his slaves from love can free,
  Nor give their thoughts repose.

They are becalm'd in clearest days,
  And in rough weather tost;
They wither under cold delays,
  Or are in tempests lost.

One while they seem to touch the port,
  Then straight into the main
Some angry wind in cruel sport
  Their vessel drives again.

At first disdain and pride they fear,
  Which, if they chance to 'scape,
Rivals and falsehood soon appear
  In a more dreadful shape.

By such degrees to joy they come,
  And are so long withstood,
So slowly they receive the sum,
  It hardly does them good.

II. SONG. "There was a poison in his love poems; but it
was a poison that enchanted the wits of the day."— Thompson, *The Literature of Society*, Vol. 1, p. 375.

'Tis cruel to prolong a pain;
  And to defer a bliss,
Believe me, gentle Hermione,
  No less inhuman is.

An hundred thousand oaths your fears
  Perhaps would not remove,
And if I gazed a thousand years,
  I could no deeper love.

III

PHYLLIS KNOTTING

" Hears not my Phyllis how the birds
  Their feathered mates salute?
They tell their passion in their words:
  Must I alone be mute? "
    Phyllis, without frown or smile,
    Sat and knotted all the while.

" The god of love in thy bright eyes
  Does like a tyrant reign;
But in thy heart a child he lies
  Without his dart or flame."
    Phyllis, without frown or smile,
    Sat and knotted all the while.

" So many months in silence past,
  And yet in raging love,
Might well deserve one word at last
  My passion should approve."
    Phyllis, without frown or smile,
    Sat and knotted all the while.

III. *Knotting.* A kind of fancy-work, somewhat like lace-making.

"Must then your faithful swain expire
And not one look obtain,
Which he to soothe his fond desire
Might pleasingly explain?"
Phyllis, without frown or smile,
Sat and knotted all the while!

IV

PHYLLIS IS MY ONLY JOY

Phyllis is my only joy,
Faithless as the winds or seas,
Sometimes coming, sometimes coy,
Yet she never fails to please;
If with a frown
I am cast down,
Phyllis, smiling
And beguiling,
Makes me happier than before.

Though, alas! too late I find
Nothing can her fancy fix,
Yet the moment she is kind
I forgive her all her tricks;
Which though I see,
I can't get free.
She deceiving,
I believing,
What need lovers wish for more?

IV. PHYLLIS IS MY ONLY JOY. "[He] has been preserved
from oblivion by a little wanton verse about Phyllis, full of
such good-natured contentment and disbelief that we grow
young and cheerful again in contemplating it."— Repplier,
English Love-Songs, Points of View.

WORKS BY THE CAVALIER POETS

WORKS BY THE CAVALIER POETS

THOMAS CAREW
　Collected Poems, ed. Hazlitt, 1870; Ebsworth, 1893;
　　　Vincent, 1899
　Caelum Britannicum, 1633
　Poems, 1640

WILLIAM CARTWRIGHT
　Comedies, Tragi-Comedies, and Other Poems, 1647,
　　　1651·

JOHN CLEVELAND
　The King's Disguise, 1646.
　Poems, 1656
　The Rustic Rampant, 1658
　Poems, Orations, and Epistles, 1660
　Poems, 1677

CHARLES COTTON
　Many poems reprinted in Chalmers' *English Poets,*
　　　1810
　Scarronides, 1664, 1670
　Tr. Corneille's *Horace,* 1671
　Voyage to Ireland in Burlesque, 1670
　Tr. Gerard's *Life of the Duke of Espernon,* 1670
　*Tr. Commentaries of De Montiac, Marshal of
　　　France,* 1674
　Second part of Walton's *Complete Angler,* 1676
　Tr. Montaigne's *Essays,* 1685
　Poems on Several Occasions, 1689

ABRAHAM COWLEY
　Collected Works, ed. Sprat, 1668, 1689, 1721; ed.
　　　Grosart, 1880
　Poetical Blossoms, 1633

Sylva, 1636
Love's Riddle, 1638
Naufragium Joculare, 1638
The Puritan and the Papist, 1643
Ad Populum, 1644
The Mistress, 1647
The Four Ages of England, 1648
The Guardian, 1650
Poems, 1656
Ode Upon the Blessed Restoration, 1660
Cromwell the Wicked, 1661
*A Proposal for the Advancement of Experimental
    Philosophy,* 1661
Several Discourses, 1661
A. Couleii Plantarum libri duo, 1662
Verses Upon Several Occasions, 1663
Verses Lately Written, 1663
The Cutter of Coleman Street, 1663
A Poem on the Late Civil War, 1679
Tr. Anacreon, 1683
Love's Chronicle (?), 1730

RICHARD CRASHAW
    Collected Works, ed. Turnbull, 1858; Grosart, 1872;
        Tutin, 1893
    Epigrammatum Sacroium Liber, 1634, 1670
    Steps to the Temple, 1646
    Carmen Deo Nostro, 1652

WILLIAM DAVENANT
    Collected Works, ed. his widow, 1673; Lang and
        Maidment, 1872-1874
    The Tragedy of Albovine, 1630
    The Cruel Brother, 1630
    The Just Italien, 1630
    The Temple of Love, 1634
    The Triumphs of the Prince d'Amour, 1635
    The Platonic Lovers, 1636
    The Wits, 1636

Britannia Triumphans, 1637
Madagascar, 1638
Ode in Remembrance of Master Shakespeare, 1638
Salmacida Spolia, 1639
To the House of Commons, 1641
The Unfortunate Lovers, 1643
London, 1643
Love and Honor, 1649
Gondibert, 1651
The Siege of Rhodes, 1656, 1663
First Dayes Entertainment at Rutland House, 1657
Cruelty of the Spaniards in Peru, 1658
History of Sir Francis Drake, 1659
Poem to the King's Most Sacred Majesty, 1660
*Poem Upon His Sacred Majesty's Most Happy
    Return,* 1660
The Rivals, 1668
The Man's the Master, 1669
The Tempest, 1670
New Academy of Compliments, 1671
Macbeth with Alterations, 1673

WILLIAM HABINGTON
  Poems reprinted in Chalmers' *English Poets,* 1810;
      ed. Gutch, 1812; Arber, 1870
  Castara, 1634, 1635, 1642
  History of Edward IV, 1640
  Queen of Aragon, 1640
  Observations Upon History, 1641

GEORGE HERBERT
  Numerous English and American Editions.   Grosart,
      1874; Shorthouse, 1882
  Parentalia, 1627
  *Oratio, qua . . . Principis Caroli Reditum ex His-
      panüs Celebravit Georgius Herbert,* 1633
  The Temple, 1633
  Jacula Prudentum, 1651 (Published as *Outlandish
      Proverbs* in *Wit's Recreations,* 1640)

Herbert's Remains, 1652
Musae Responsoriae, 1662
Tr. Cornaro's *Treatise on Temperance,* 1634
Tr. de Valdes' *Hundred and Ten Considerations,*
    1638
ROBERT HERRICK
    Collected Works, ed. Lord Dundrennan, 1823; Haz-
        litt, 1869; Grosart, 1876; Palgrave, 1877; Pol-
        lard, 1891; Saintsbury, 1893; Hale, Rhys,
        Singer, etc.
    King Obron's Feast, 1635
    His Mistris Shade, 1640
    Hesperides (with *Noble Numbers,* 1647), 1648
    Poems in *Lacrymae Musarum,* 1649, and *Wit's
        Recreations,* 1650
RICHARD LOVELACE
    Collected Works, ed. Hazlitt, 1864.
    The Scholar: A Comedy, 1634
    The Soldier: A Tragedy, 1640
    Lucasta, 1649
    Posthume Poems, 1659
ANDREW MARVELL
    Collected Works, ed. Cooke, 1726; Thompson, 1776;
        Grosart, 1875; Aitken, 1892
    The First Anniversary of the Government, 1655
    The Character of Holland, 1665
    Clarendon's House-Warming, 1667
    The Rehearsal Transposed, 1672, 1673
    An Apology and Advice for Some of the Clergy,
        1674
    Dialogue between Two Horses, 1675
    Plain Dealing, 1675
    Mr. Smirke, 1676
    A Seasonable Question, 1676
    The Growth of Popery, 1677
    A Seasonable Argument, 1678
    Remarks upon a Disengenuous Discourse, 1678

A Short Historical Essay touching General Councils, 1680
Miscellaneous Poems, 1681
Characters of Popery, 1689
Poems on Affairs of State, 1689
The Royal Manual, 1751
Poems in various popular collections of the day.

FRANCIS QUARLES
Collected Works, ed. Grosart, 1881; *Emblems,* ed. Gilfillan.
Argalus and Parthenia, 1621
Emblems Divine and Moral, 1635
Enchiridion, 1640

CHARLES SEDLEY
Earl of Pembroke's Speech, 1648
Last Will and Testament of the Earl of Pembroke, 1650
The Mulberry Garden, 1668
Antony and Cleopatra, 1671
Bellamira, 1687
Beauty the Conqueror, 1702
The Grumbler, 1702
The Tyrant King of Crete, 1702
The Happy Pair, 1702
Plays, Poems, Songs, Etc., 1702
Collected Works, 1707, 1778

CHARLES SACKVILLE
Selections in *Poems on Several Occasions,* 1701, and in *Works of Celebrated Authors,* 1750

EDWARD SHERBURNE
Poems reprinted in Chalmers' *English Poets,* 1810
Salmasis, Lyrian, and Sylvia, 1651
Tr. *Sphere of Menilius*
Tr. Theocritus' *Sixteenth Idyllium*
Tr. Seneca's *Tragedies*

THOMAS STANLEY
Collected poems, ed. Brydges, 1814

Poems and Translations, 1647
Poems by T. S., 1651
History of Philosophy, 1655-1662
Ed. Aeschylus, 1663
Commentaries on Aeschylus
Adversaria
Prelections on the Characters of Theophrastus
Tr. Anacreon

SIR JOHN SUCKLING
Collected Works, ed. A. Suckling, 1836; Hazlitt, 1874, 1893; Stokes, 1885
A Session of Poets, 1637
Aglaura, 1638
Ballad on a Wedding, 1640
Fragmenta Aurea, 1646
The Goblins, published in *Fragmenta Aurea,* 1646
Brennoralt, published in *Fragmenta Aurea,* 1646
The Sad One, 1658
Last Remains, 1659
Letters to Divers Eminent Personages
An Account of Religion by Reason

HENRY VAUGHAN
Collected Works, ed. Grosart; Poems, ed. Chambers, 1896
Secular Poems, 1646
Tr. Tenth Satire of Juvenal, 1646
Silex Scintillans, 1650, 1656
Olor Iscanus, 1651
Mount of Olives, 1652
Thalia Rediviva, 1678
Flores Solitudinis, 1678

EDMUND WALLER
Collected Works, ed. Drury, 1893.
Four Speeches in the House of Commons, 1641
Speech . . . 4 July, 1643, 1643
Poems, 1645
Panegyrick to My Lord Protector, 1655

Upon the Late Storm and Death of His Highness,
  1658
To the King, 1660
Poem on St. James Park, 1661
To My Lady Morton, 1661
To the Queen, 1663
Pompey the Great, 1664
Upon Her Majesty's New Buildings, 1665
Instructions to a Painter, 1666
The Maid's Tragedy Altered, 1690
Poems, 1690

DR. JOHN WILSON

Airs to a Voice Alone (in *Select Airs and Dia-
  logues*), 1653
Psalterium Carolinum, 1657
Cheerful Airs and Ballads, 1660
Divine Services and Anthems, 1663
MS. Volume in Bodleian Library

GEORGE WITHER

Collected Poems, ed. Morley, 1891; Spenser Society,
  1870-1883
Prince Henry's Obsequies, 1612
Epithalamia, 1612
Abuses Stript and Whipt, 1613
A Satyre, 1614
The Shepherds Hunting, 1615
Fidelia, 1617
The Motto, 1618
A Preparation to the Psalter, 1619
Works, 1620
Exercises upon the First Psalm, 1620
The Songs of the Old Testament, 1621
The Mistress of Philarete, 1622
Juveniliae, 1622,
Faire-Virtue, 1622
The Hymns and Songs of the Church, 1623
The Scholar's Purgatory, 1625

Britain's Remembrancer, 1628
Psalms of David, 1632
Emblems, 1634-1635
Tr. *Nemesius' Nature of Man,* 1636
Read and Wonder, 1641
Hallelujah, 1641
Campo-Musae, 1643
Se Defendo, 1643
Mercurius Rusticus, 1643
The Speech Without Door, 1644
The Two Incomparable Generalissimos, 1644
Letters of Advice, 1645
Vox Pacifica, 1645
The Speech Without Door Defended, 1646
Justiciarus Justificatus, 1646
What Peace to the Wicked, 1646
Opobalsamum Anglicanum, 1646
Major Wither's Disclaimer, 1647
Carmen Expostulatorium, 1647
Amygdale Britannica, 1647
Prosopopaeia Britannica, 1648
Carmen Eucharisticon, 1649
Respublica Anglicana, 1650
The British Appeals, 1651
Three Grains of Spiritual Frankincense, 1651
The Dark Lantern, 1653
Westrow Revived, 1653
Vaticinum Casuale, 1655
Rapture at the Protector's Recovery, 1655
Three Private Meditations, 1655
The Protector, 1655
Boni Ominis Votum, 1656
A Suddain Flash, 1657
Salt upon Salt, 1659
A Cordial Confection, 1659
Epistolium Vagum-Prosa-Metricum, 1659

Petition and Narrative, 1659
Furor Poeticus, 1660
Speculum Speculativum, 1660
Fides Anglicana, 1660
An Improvement of Imprisonment, 1661
A Triple Paradox, 1661
The Prisoner's Plea, 1661
A Proclamation in the Name of the King of Kings,
    1662
Tuba Pacifica, 1664
A Memorandum to London, 1665
Meditations upon the Lord's Prayer, 1665
Echoes from the Sixth Trumpet, 1666
Sighs for the Pitchers, 1666
Vaticina Poetica, 1666
Divine Poems on the Ten Commandments, 1688

BIBLIOGRAPHY

BIBLIOGRAPHY

Aitkin: *Memoirs of the Court of King Charles I*
Addison: *An Account of the Greatest English Poets*
Alcott: *Concord Days*
Aldrich: *Poems of Robert Herrick*
Allibone: *Dictionary of English Literature*
American Journal of Philology
Anderson: *British Poets*
Angus: *Handbook of English Literature*
Arber: *English Garner*
Arnold: *Chaucer to Wordsworth*
Ashe: "Robert Herrick," *Temple Bar*, Vol. LXVIII
Ashton: *Social Life in the Reign of Queen Anne*
Aubrey: *Brief Lives*
Bagehot: *Literary Studies*
Baker: *Chronicle of the Kings of England*
Baxter: *Poetical Fragments*
Beattie: *Essay on Poetry and Music*
Behn: *On the Death of Waller*
Bell: *Songs from the Dramatists*
Benson: *Essays*
Biographica Britannica
Blair: *Lectures on Rhetoric and Belles Lettres*
Brand: *Popular Antiquities*
Brook: *English Literature*
Brown: "The Parson of Bemerton," *Good Words*, Vol.
 XXXI
Brown: "Vaughan's Poems," *North British Review*,
 Vol. II
Browning (Eliz): *The Book of the Poets*
Browning: *Letters of Robert Browning and Elizabeth
 Barrett*

303

Browning: *Letters*
Brydges: *Censura Literaria*
Bullen: *More Lyrics from Elizabethan Song Books*
Bullen: *Musa Proterva*
Burd: *Commonplace Book*
Burnet: *History of My Own Times*
Burroughs: "On the Reading of Books," *The Century,* Vol. LX
Buxton: "Marvell," *Gentleman's Magazine,* Vol. CCXXXI
Cambridge History of English Literature
Campbell: *Specimens of the British Poets*
Carpenter: *English Lyric Poetry*
Cartwright: *Sacharissa*
Casserly: "A Cavalier Poet of the Seventeenth Century," *American Catholic Monthly Review,* Vol. II, p. 614.
Century Cyclopedia of Names
Chambers: *Biographical Dictionary*
Chambers: *Cyclopaedia of English Literature*
Chalmers: *English Poets*
Churchill: *The Author*
Churchill: *The Apology*
Cibber: *Lives of the Poets*
Clarendon (Lord): *Life*
Cleveland: *A Compendium of English Literature*
Coleridge (H): *Biographia Borealis*
Coleridge: *Biographia Literaria*
Coleridge: *Lectures and Notes on Shakespeare*
Coleridge: *Letters and Conversation*
Coleridge: *Style, Miscellanies, Etc.*
Coleridge (Sara): *Memoirs and Letters*
Collins: *Essays and Studies*
Collins: *Voltaire in England*
Congreve: *The Old Bachelor*
Courthope: *History of English Poetry*

Cowley: *On the Death of Mr. Crashaw*
Cowper: *The Task*
Craik: *Compendious History of English Literature*
Craik: *English Prose*
Crawfurd: *Lyrical Verse from Elizabeth to Victoria*
Creasy: *Memoirs of Eminent Etonians*
Cunningham: *Ben Jonson*
Daniel: *A Vindication of Poesy*
Dennis: *Age of Pope*
Dennis: *Heroes of Literature*
Dennis: *Letters*
De Quincey: *Historical Essays*
Dictionary of National Biography
Disraeli: *Quarrels of Authors*
Dobson: " In a Copy of the Lyrical Poems of Robert
    Herrick," *Scribner's*, Vol. I
Dove: *Life of Marvell*
Dowden: *Outlines of the Theological Literature of the
    Church of England*
Drake: *Literary Hours*
Drake: *Shakespeare and His Times*
Dryden: *Critical and Miscellaneous Essays*
Dryden: Dedication of *The Assignation*
Dryden: *Essay on Dramatic Poetry*
Dryden: *Essay on Heroic Plays*
Dryden: *Essay on Satire*
Dryden: Preface to *Fables*
Duffield: " Henry Vaughan," *Presbyterian Review*,
    Vol. I
Egan: *Lectures on English Literature*
Egan: " Three Catholic Poets," *Catholic World*, Vol.
    XXXII
Ellis: *Specimens of the Early English Poets*
Elze: *Essays on Shakespeare*
Emerson: Preface to *Parnassus*
Emery: *Notes on English Literature*
Encyclopaedia Britannica

Field: "Select Poems from Herrick, Carew, etc."
    Quarterly Review, Vol. IV
Fivie: "George Wither," *Macmillan's Magazine*, Vol.
    LXII
Fleay: *Biographical Chronicle of the English Drama*
Flecknoe: *Short Discourse on the English Stage*
Freswell: *Essays on English Writers*
Frey: *Sobriquets and Nicknames*
Fuller: *The Worthies of England*
Gay: *On a Miscellany of Poems*
Gardner: *History of England from the Accession of
    James I to the Outbreak of the Civil War*
Gifford: *The Works of Ben Jonson*
Gilfillan: *Specimens of the Less-known British Poets*
Goldsmith: *The Bee*, Vol. VIII
Goldsmith: *The Beauties of England*
Gosse: *From Shakespeare to Pope*
Gosse: *History of Eighteenth Century Literature*
Gosse: *Jacobean Poets*
Gosse: *Seventeenth Century Studies*
Gosse: *Short History of Modern English Literature*
Granger: *Biographical History of England*
Green: *Short History of English People*
Grosart: *Fuller Worthies' Miscellanies*
Grosart: "George Herbert," *Leisure Hours*, Vol. XXII
Guiney: *A Little English Gallery*
Guiney: *A Roadside Harp*
Hale: *Die Chronologische Anordnung der Dichtungen
    Robert Herricks* (Dissertation, Halle, 1892)
Hall: *Book of Gems*
Hall: *Pilgrimages to English Shrines*
Hallam: *Introduction to the Literature of Europe*
Hannah: *Courtly Poets*
Hannay: *Essays for the Quarterly Review*
Hart: *A Manual of English Literature*
Hawkins: *History of Music*
Hazlitt: *Lectures on the English Comic Writers*

Hazlitt: *Lectures on the Literature of the Age of Elizabeth*
Headley: *Select Beauties of Ancient English Poetry*
Hearne: *Reliquiae Hearnianae,* ed. Bliss
Henley: *Views and Reviews*
Horner: *Memoirs and Correspondence*
Hume: *History of England*
Hunt: *Men, Women, and Books*
Hunt: *The Town*
Hunt: *Table-Talk*
Hunt: *Wit and Humor*
Hutton: Literary Landmarks of London
Hutton: *Social England*
Imperial Dictionary of Universal Biography
International Encyclopaedia
Jameson: *The Loves of the Poets*
Jesse: *Memoirs of the Court of England during the Reign of the Stuarts*
Johnson: *Lives of the English Poets*
Johnson: *Outline History of English and American Literature*
Kingsley: *Plays and Puritans, Miscellanies*
Lamb: *George Wither's Poetical Works*
Lamb: *Letters*
Lang: *Letters on Literature*
Langbaine: *The English Dramatic Poets*
Langford: *Prison Books and their Authors*
Lawrence: *English Literature Periods, Classical Period*
Leisure Hours
Linton: *Rare Poems of the Sixteenth and Seventeenth Centuries*
Lloyd: *Memoirs of Excellent Personages*
Locker-Lampson: *My Confidences*
Lowell: *Among My Books*
Lowell: *Library of Old Authors, Prose Works,* Vol. II
Lowell: *On a Certain Condescension in Foreigners*

Lytton: *St. Stephen's*
Macaulay: *Catherine Sedley, Historical and Critical Essays*
Macaulay: *Milton*
MacDonald: *England's Antiphon*
Manchester: *Court and Society from Elizabeth to Anne*
Masson: *Life of John Milton*
Masterman: *Age of Milton*
Milton: *Letters*
Minto: *Manual of English Prose Literature*
Mitchell: *English Lands, Letters, and Kings*
Mitford: *Recollections of a Literary Life*
Morley: *First Book of Madrigals*
Morley: *The King and the Commons*
Morley: *Universal Library*
Morrill: *Self-Consciousness of Noted Persons*
Morris (Sir Lewis): " To An Unknown Poet," *Songs of Two Worlds, Second Series*
Neele: *Lectures on English Poetry*
Notes and Queries
Painter: *History of English Literature*
Palgrave: *Golden Treasury*
Palgrave: *Landscape in Poetry*
Palgrave: " Robert Herrick," *Macmillan's Magazine,* Vol. XXXV
Palgrave: *Treasury of Sacred Songs*
Pancoast: *Standard English Poems*
Park: *Wit's Recreations*
Pattison: *Life of Milton*
Pearson: *Brome's Plays*
Pepys': *Diary*
Percy: *Reliques of Ancient English Poetry*
Perry: *History of the Church of England*
Phillips: *Theatrum Poetarum Anglicanorum*
Pollard: " Herrick and His Friends," *Macmillan's Magazine,* Vol. LXIX

Pope: *Dunciad*
Pope: *Epistle to Augustus*
Pope: *First Epistle of the Second Book of Horace*
Pope: *Letters*
Preston: " The Latest Songs of Chivalry," *Atlantic Monthly*, Vol. XLIII
Publications of the Modern Language Association
Publications of the Spenser Society
Raleigh: *The English Novel*
Rees: *Encyclopaedia of Arts and Sciences*
Repplier: *English Love-Songs, Points of View*
Rice: " Edmund Waller," *North American Review*, Vol. XCI
Robertson: *Children of the Poets*
Robertson: *History of English Literature*
Rochester: *An Allusion to the Tenth Satire of the First Book of Horace*
Rogers: " Andrew Marvell," *Edinburgh Review*, Vol. LXXIX
Rossetti: *Humorous Poems*
Ruffhead: *Life of Pope*
Rymer: *A Short View of the Tragedy of the Last Age*
Saintsbury: *History of English Literature*
Sanders: " Robert Herrick," *Gentleman's Magazine*, Vol. CCLXXX
Saunders: *Evenings with the Sacred Poets*
Schegel: *Dramatic Art and Literature*
Schelling: *Book of Elizabethan Lyrics*
Schelling: *Book of Seventeenth Century Songs*
Schelling: *Poetic and Verse Criticism of the Reign of Elizabeth*
Scherr: *History of English Literature*
Scoones: *Four Centuries of English Letters*
Scollard: " A Forgotten Poet," *The Dial*, Vol. XIV
Scott: *Life of John Dryden*
Shadwell: *A True Widow*
Smith: *English Fugitive Poets, Poets and Novelists*

Smith: "Sir John Suckling," *Gentleman's Magazine,* Vol. CCXLIII

Soame: *The Art of Poetry*

Sothern: "Vaughan's *Olor Iscanus,*" *Retrospective Review,* Vol. III

Southey: *Lives of Uneducated Poets*

Spence's Anecdotes, ed. Singer

Stockdale: *Life of Waller*

Suckling (Sir John): *Sessions of the Poets*

Swinburne: *Studies in Prose and Poetry*

Tabley: *Poems, Dramatic and Lyric*

Taine: *History of English Literature*

Thompson: *The Literature of Society*

Thompson: *The Wits and Beaux of Society*

Thoreau: *Familiar Letters,* ed. Sanborn

Thorne: *Hand-Book of the Environs of London*

Tovey: *Reviews and Essays in English Literature*

Traill: *Social England*

Trench: *Household Book of English Poetry*

Tullock: *Rational Theology and Christian Philosophy in England in the Seventeenth Century*

Vaughan: Preface, *Silex Scientillans*

Waite: "Richard Lovelace," *Gentleman's Magazine,* Vol. CCLVII

Walpole: *Catalogue of the Royal and Noble Authors of England, Scotland, and Ireland*

Walpole: *Letters,* ed. Cunningham

Walton: *Lives*

Ward: *English Poets*

Ward: *History of English Dramatic Literature*

Warner: *Library of the World's Best Literature*

Welch: "In an Ancient Copy of Herrick's Hesperides," *Century Magazine,* Vol. LI

West: *The Laureates of England*

Whipple: *Authors in Their Relation to Life*

Whipple: *Essays and Reviews*

Whipple: *Literature and Life*

Whipple: *Literature of the Age of Elizabeth*
Whittier: *Old Portraits and Modern Sketches*
Willmott: *The Works of George Herbert*
Winstanley: *Lives of the Most Famous English Poets*
Wood: *Athenae Oxonienses*
Wordsworth: Preface, *Lyrical Ballads*

INDEX OF AUTHORS AND SELECTIONS

INDEX OF FIRST LINES